EXPERIENCE BORA BORA: A TRAVEL PREPARATION GUIDE.

DELZY HAMPTON

TABLE OF CONTENTS

INTRODUCTION

Escape to the breathtaking beauty of Bora Bora, where turquoise waters stretch as far as the eye can see, and lush green peaks rise majestically from the Pacific Ocean. This alluring travel guide is your key to unlocking the secrets of this idyllic tropical paradise, as we take you on a journey of discovery through this gem of French Polynesia.

"EXPERIENCE BORA BORA " is a comprehensive travel companion that caters to every adventurer seeking the perfect island escape. Whether you're a honeymooning couple yearning for romantic seclusion or an adrenaline junkie in pursuit of thrilling water sports, this guide has something to offer everyone.

Discover the island's rich history, deeply rooted in Polynesian culture and traditions. Immerse yourself in the warm hospitality of the locals, who will welcome you with open arms and share their stories of ancient myths and legends.

Indulge in the ultimate luxury of overwater bungalows perched above crystal-clear lagoons, providing uninterrupted views of the surrounding natural wonders. Savor the mouth watering delicacies of Polynesian cuisine, infused with fresh seafood and tropical fruits.

For those seeking adventure, "experience Bora Bora" presents an array of exhilarating activities, from snorkeling among vibrant coral reefs teeming with marine life to diving with majestic manta rays and sharks. Discover hidden coves and secluded beaches on thrilling island-hopping escapades.

Navigate the island's vibrant markets and boutique shops, where you can find unique souvenirs and handicrafts made by local artisans. Unearth the best spots for mesmerizing sunsets and enjoy evenings filled with lively dance performances and enchanting fire shows.

In "experience Bora Bora" we leave no stone unturned, ensuring you have all the essential information and tips for a seamless and unforgettable vacation. So pack your bags, escape the ordinary, and embark on an adventure of a lifetime in the mesmerizing wonderland that is Bora Bora.

WHY VISIT BORA BORA

In the vast expanse of the Pacific Ocean lies a gem of untold beauty and allure - Bora Bora. This idyllic island in French Polynesia has long captured the imagination of travelers from across the globe, beckoning them with its pristine white-sand beaches, crystalline turquoise waters, and lush tropical landscapes. A visit to Bora Bora is not merely a vacation; it is a transformative experience that stirs the soul and leaves an indelible mark on the heart. In this section, we will explore the myriad reasons why Bora Bora should be on every traveler's bucket list, encompassing its natural wonders, vibrant culture, thrilling activities, luxurious accommodations, and the deep sense of tranquility it offers to those who set foot on its shores.

Natural Wonders: Bora Bora is renowned for its unparalleled natural beauty. The island's iconic image of a central emerald peak surrounded by a ring of azure lagoon is etched in the minds of many. The extinct volcano, Mount Otemanu, rises majestically from the center of the island, providing a dramatic backdrop to the paradise below. The lagoon, teeming with colorful marine life, is ideal for snorkeling and diving, offering a glimpse into an underwater world like no other. Coral reefs encircle the island, creating a natural barrier and adding to the allure of the island's aquatic wonderland.

Turquoise Waters: The calm, clear waters surrounding Bora Bora are a true marvel. The lagoon is renowned for its varying shades of blue and turquoise, which seem almost unreal in their brilliance. It is here that visitors can find a sanctuary of peace, a place to escape the hustle and bustle of modern life and immerse themselves in the serenity of nature.

Overwater Bungalows: One of the most enchanting features of Bora Bora is its array of luxurious overwater bungalows. These iconic accommodations extend out over the lagoon, offering guests unparalleled views and direct access to the pristine waters. Staying in an overwater bungalow is a once-in-a-lifetime experience, a dream-like escape where one can wake up to the gentle lapping of waves and fall asleep under the twinkling stars.

Vibrant Culture: The culture of Bora Bora is deeply rooted in the traditions of the Polynesian people. The locals are warm, friendly, and proud of their heritage. Visitors have the opportunity to engage in traditional ceremonies, witness dance performances, and taste authentic Polynesian cuisine. Learning about the local way of life and embracing their rich cultural heritage is an integral part of any Bora Bora experience.

Water Activities: Bora Bora is a playground for water enthusiasts. Whether you prefer relaxing on a serene lagoon cruise, exploring the coral gardens on a snorkeling expedition, or embarking on a thrilling shark and ray feeding excursion, the island offers a myriad of water-based activities to suit every taste and preference.

Hiking and Nature Exploration: Beyond its aquatic wonders, Bora Bora boasts captivating landscapes that are begging to be explored. Guided hikes to Mount Pahia and Mount Otemanu offer breathtaking views of the island and surrounding waters. Nature enthusiasts will revel in the opportunity to witness endemic flora and fauna, including vibrant tropical birds and lush vegetation.

Romantic Retreat: Bora Bora is synonymous with romance, making it a dream destination for honeymooners and couples seeking an intimate getaway. The stunning sunsets, the privacy of overwater bungalows, and the sense of seclusion all contribute to an atmosphere of love and intimacy that is truly unrivaled.

Diverse Dining Experiences: Despite its small size, Bora Bora offers a diverse culinary scene. Visitors can indulge in delectable French-Polynesian fusion cuisine, fresh seafood, tropical fruits, and more. Dining experiences range from casual beachside eateries to upscale restaurants offering gourmet delights.

Unforgettable Sunsets: As the sun dips below the horizon, painting the sky with hues of pink, orange, and purple, Bora Bora treats its visitors to breathtaking sunsets that will forever be etched in their memories.

Rejuvenating Spas: For those seeking relaxation and rejuvenation, Bora Bora's world-class spas provide a haven of tranquility. Surrounded by the calming sounds of the ocean, guests can indulge in various treatments, such as traditional Polynesian massages and soothing coconut-based therapies.

Bora Bora's Motus: A trip to Bora Bora wouldn't be complete without exploring its picturesque motus. These small islets dot the lagoon and offer a unique opportunity to experience the unspoiled beauty of nature. Many resorts arrange private picnics on these islets, where visitors can enjoy a secluded day in paradise.

Water Sports Galore: Adventure-seekers will find themselves in paradise with the plethora of water sports available on the island. From jet skiing and windsurfing to paddleboarding and kiteboarding, Bora Bora offers a wide range of activities that cater to thrill-seekers.

Stargazing: The lack of light pollution on the island makes Bora Bora an ideal spot for stargazing. As night falls, the sky becomes a celestial canvas, and visitors can witness the dazzling display of stars, including the Southern Cross, in all its glory.

Conservation Efforts: Bora Bora has become increasingly focused on preserving its natural beauty and fragile ecosystem. Various initiatives are in place to protect marine life, coral reefs, and the environment, allowing visitors to witness and support these conservation efforts.

CHAPTER ONE

PLANNING YOUR TRIP

Understanding Bora Bora

Before diving into the planning process, it's essential to understand what makes Bora Bora so special. This section will provide an overview of the island's geography, culture, climate, and the best time to visit.

Bora Bora's Geography: Bora Bora is a small island located in the South Pacific Ocean, part of the Society Islands archipelago in French Polynesia. Its unique landscape features a dormant volcano at its center surrounded by a vibrant coral reef and a turquoise lagoon, creating a breathtaking setting.

Local Culture: The people of Bora Bora are welcoming and proud of their Polynesian heritage. The local culture is deeply rooted in traditional dances, music, and crafts. Respect for their customs and traditions is crucial during your stay.

Climate and Best Time to Visit: Bora Bora has a tropical climate with two distinct seasons - the wet season (November to April) and the dry season (May to October). The dry season offers the best weather for outdoor activities, making it the ideal time to visit.

2: Visa and Travel Documents

Before packing your bags, ensure you have all the necessary travel documents.

Visa Requirements: Depending on your nationality, you may need a visa to enter French Polynesia. Check the visa requirements through the official French Polynesia consulate or embassy in your country.

Passport Validity: Ensure your passport is valid for at least six months beyond your planned departure date from French Polynesia.

Other Essential Documents: Don't forget to carry travel insurance, flight tickets, hotel reservations, and any necessary medical records.

3: Booking Flights

Finding the best flight to Bora Bora is an exciting step.

Finding Flights: Start by searching for flights to Faa'a International Airport in Tahiti, as it's the main international gateway to French Polynesia. From there, you can take a domestic flight to Bora Bora Airport, which is on the Motu Mute islet.

Booking Timing: To secure the best deals, book your flights well in advance, preferably 4 to 6 months before your planned travel dates.

Flight Duration: The flight duration from major international hubs to Tahiti is usually around 8-10 hours, depending on your location. The domestic flight from Tahiti to Bora Bora takes approximately 45 minutes.

4: Choosing Accommodations

Bora Bora is famous for its luxurious overwater bungalows, but there are various accommodation options to suit different budgets and preferences.

Overwater Bungalows: For the ultimate Bora Bora experience, consider staying in an overwater bungalow. These private and luxurious villas allow you to immerse yourself in the stunning lagoon and offer direct access to the crystal-clear waters.

Beachfront Resorts: If overwater bungalows are out of your budget, beachfront resorts provide a comfortable and scenic alternative. You'll still enjoy breathtaking views and direct access to the beach.

Budget-Friendly Options: Bora Bora also offers some budget-friendly accommodations, such as guesthouses and family-run lodges. While they may not have all the luxury amenities, they provide a more authentic and affordable experience.

5: Planning Activities and Excursions

With its idyllic surroundings, Bora Bora offers a plethora of activities and excursions to make your trip unforgettable.

Water Activities: Embrace the island's aquatic wonders by indulging in activities like snorkeling, scuba diving, jet skiing, paddleboarding, and shark and stingray feeding.

Island Exploration: Take a guided tour to explore the heart of the island, including Mount Otemanu and lush hiking trails that offer breathtaking panoramic views.

Cultural Experiences: Immerse yourself in the local culture by attending traditional dance performances, visiting local markets, and engaging with the warm and friendly residents.

6: Dining in Bora Bora

Bora Bora boasts an array of culinary delights, ranging from fresh seafood to traditional Polynesian dishes.

Local Cuisine: Sample traditional dishes like Poisson Cru (raw fish marinated in coconut milk and lime), Roulottes (food trucks), and a variety of tropical fruits.

Fine Dining: The island also hosts a selection of upscale restaurants that offer gourmet experiences with stunning views of the lagoon.

Romantic Dinners: Many resorts arrange private dining experiences on the beach or in your overwater bungalow, creating unforgettable romantic moments.

7: Budgeting and Expenses

Bora Bora is renowned for its luxury, but it is possible to enjoy this paradise on a reasonable budget with proper planning.

Accommodation: Accommodation costs can vary significantly, depending on your choice of lodging. Set your budget and research accordingly.

Meals and Dining: Plan for meals in advance and consider including some budget-friendly options along with a few special dining experiences.

Activities and Excursions: Research the costs of activities and prioritize the ones you'd like to do most.

Souvenirs and Shopping: Allocate a separate budget for souvenirs and shopping, as Bora Bora offers unique crafts and local products.

8: Packing Tips

To make the most of your Bora Bora trip, pack strategically and efficiently.

Clothing: Light and breathable clothing, swimwear, sunscreen, sunglasses, and a wide-brimmed hat are essential.

Underwater Gear: Bring your snorkeling gear if you have it, but if not, many resorts provide complimentary equipment.

Medications and First Aid: Carry essential medications and a basic first-aid kit, including insect repellent.

Best Time to Visit

The best time to visit this idyllic destination largely depends on various factors, including weather, crowds, and personal preferences.

- **Understanding Bora Bora's Climate:** Before delving into the best time to visit, it's crucial to understand Bora Bora's climate. The island experiences a tropical, maritime climate with two main seasons: the wet season (November to April) and the dry season (May to October). During the wet season, visitors can expect higher humidity, occasional heavy rainfall, and the possibility of tropical storms and cyclones. On the other hand, the dry season offers pleasant weather with lower humidity and minimal rainfall.

- **Peak Tourist Season:** May to October Bora Bora's peak tourist season coincides with the dry season, which runs from May to October. This period is characterized by clear skies, balmy temperatures, and lower chances of rain. As a result, visitors can enjoy outdoor activities like snorkeling, scuba diving, and exploring the island without worrying about the weather.

- **Weather in the Dry Season:** The dry season showcases the best weather on the island, making it the preferred time for many travelers. During these months, daytime temperatures typically range from 25°C to 30°C (77°F to 86°F), with cooler evenings. The calm and sunny weather is perfect for lounging on the beautiful beaches and taking advantage of the vibrant marine life in the lagoon.

- **Bora Bora's Off-Peak Season:** November to April The wet season, which extends from November to April, is Bora Bora's off-peak season. During this time, the island experiences occasional rain showers and increased humidity. While it is the least popular time to visit due to the higher chances of rainfall, it still attracts some travelers who prefer fewer crowds and more affordable accommodations.

- **Whale Watching:** July to November If you are a fan of marine life and dream of witnessing majestic creatures, the months from July to November are a delightful time to visit Bora Bora. During this period, humpback whales migrate to the warm waters of French Polynesia to breed and give birth. Tourists have the opportunity to embark on whale-watching tours to witness these incredible creatures in their natural habitat.

- **Crowd Factors:** The number of tourists on Bora Bora varies throughout the year. The peak season (May to October) attracts a larger influx of visitors, which may lead to higher accommodation rates and more crowded attractions. In contrast, the off-peak season (November to April) sees fewer tourists, making it an excellent choice for those seeking a more tranquil and intimate experience.

- **Booking and Accommodation:** To ensure availability and potentially secure better rates, it's recommended to book accommodations well in advance, especially during the peak season. Many resorts on the island offer luxurious overwater bungalows, which are popular among visitors for their direct access to the turquoise lagoon and breathtaking views.

- **Festivals and Events:** The timing of your visit can also align with unique festivals and events that showcase Bora Bora's vibrant culture. For example, Heiva, a traditional Polynesian festival, takes place in July and features traditional dance performances, sports competitions, and craft markets.

- **Scuba Diving and Snorkeling:** Bora Bora is a haven for underwater enthusiasts, and the visibility is generally excellent year-round. However, if you are seeking optimal conditions for scuba diving and snorkeling, the dry season offers better visibility and calmer waters, enhancing your chances of encountering various marine species, including rays, sharks, and tropical fish.

- **Romantic Escapes:** Bora Bora is a popular destination for honeymooners and couples seeking a romantic getaway. The peak season's idyllic weather and stunning sunsets make it an ideal time for those looking to celebrate their love in a paradisiacal setting.

Travel Essentials

When planning a trip to Bora Bora, it's essential to pack wisely to ensure a comfortable and enjoyable stay.

1. Travel Documents

Before embarking on your journey to Bora Bora, make sure you have all the necessary travel documents ready. This includes a valid passport with at least six months validity from the date of entry, travel insurance, and any required visas. Ensure you keep multiple copies of these documents in different bags and a digital backup on your phone or email.

2. Clothing

Bora Bora's climate is tropical, so lightweight and breathable clothing are essential. Pack items like swimwear, shorts, tank tops, sundresses, and lightweight shirts. Don't forget to include a few dressier options for elegant dining experiences, as some restaurants may have a smart-casual dress code. A wide-brimmed hat, sunglasses, and a sarong or cover-up for the beach are also practical additions. Although the weather is warm, it's crucial to bring a light jacket or sweater for cooler evenings or air-conditioned spaces.

3. Footwear

Bora Bora is a destination where you'll spend a lot of time outdoors, so comfortable footwear is a must. Bring sandals or flip-flops for the beach and walking shoes or hiking sandals for exploring the island's trails and nature. If you plan to engage in water activities like snorkeling or scuba diving, water shoes are useful to protect your feet from coral and rocks.

4. Sun Protection

The sun in Bora Bora can be intense, so sun protection is paramount. Pack sunscreen with a high SPF rating, preferably waterproof, to shield your skin from harmful UV rays. Aloe vera gel or after-sun lotion is also handy in case of sunburn. Additionally, carry a wide-brimmed hat and sunglasses to protect your face and eyes from the sun.

5. Insect Repellent

While Bora Bora is a paradise, it is still a tropical destination with mosquitoes and other insects. Pack a reliable insect repellent containing DEET or other recommended ingredients to avoid bug bites, especially during the evening and early morning.

6. Travel Adapters and Chargers

French Polynesia uses Type E sockets with a voltage of 220V, so if you're traveling from a country with a different socket type or voltage, be sure to bring the appropriate travel adapter and charger for your electronic devices.

7. Medications and First-Aid Kit

Pack any essential medications you may need during your trip, along with a basic first-aid kit that includes band-aids, antiseptic cream, pain relievers, motion sickness tablets, and any other personal medical items you require.

8. Cash and Cards

While Bora Bora does have ATMs and credit card facilities in most hotels and popular areas, it's still advisable to carry some cash for small purchases or in case of emergencies. Notify your bank of your travel plans to ensure your credit/debit cards work smoothly during your stay.

9. Reusable Water Bottle and Snorkeling Gear

Bora Bora's tap water is generally safe to drink, so bring a reusable water bottle to stay hydrated and minimize plastic waste. If you have your snorkeling gear, consider packing it to explore the vibrant marine life right from your overwater bungalow or on snorkeling excursions.

10. Electronics and Camera

Don't forget your camera or smartphone to capture the breathtaking beauty of Bora Bora. With stunning landscapes and mesmerizing sunsets, you'll want to preserve these memories. Remember to bring extra memory cards and chargers to avoid any disappointments.

11. Waterproof Bag or Dry Bag

A waterproof bag or dry bag is ideal for protecting your valuables and electronics while engaging in water activities or if unexpected rain showers occur.

12. Travel Guide and Maps

Even though Bora Bora is a relatively small island, having a travel guide or maps can be helpful for navigating and discovering the best places to visit, dine, and explore.

13. Snacks and Water Activities Equipment

Snacks, especially energy bars, can come in handy during excursions or when you're out exploring and might not have easy access to food. If you have specific water activities equipment like paddleboards or water sports gear you enjoy, you might want to bring them along, though many resorts offer rentals.

14. Language Basics

Although English is spoken in most tourist areas, it's always appreciated by the locals if you make an effort to learn a few basic French or Tahitian phrases. Simple greetings and polite expressions can go a long way in enhancing your travel experience.

15. Travel Locks and Security

To ensure the safety of your belongings, bring travel locks for your suitcases and bags. Many resorts also provide in-room safes for added security.

Passport and Visa Requirements

Passport Requirements

To enter Bora Bora, travelers must possess a valid passport. It is essential to consider the following aspects:

Types of Passports

Most countries issue regular tourist passports for their citizens, valid for international travel. Some countries offer diplomatic, official, or emergency passports, each with specific purposes and privileges. Ensure you possess the appropriate type of passport before traveling.

Validity and Expiration

For entry to Bora Bora, your passport must be valid for at least six months beyond your intended stay. This requirement ensures that visitors have sufficient validity to accommodate their entire visit.

Passport Renewal and Replacement

If your passport is nearing its expiration or has already expired, it is advisable to renew it before traveling to Bora Bora. Many countries have expedited renewal services, but it is best to apply for a new passport well in advance to avoid last-minute complications.

Visa Requirements

French Polynesia, including Bora Bora, operates under specific visa regulations. The requirements vary depending on your nationality, the purpose of your visit, and the duration of your stay. Below are some common visa types:

Visa-Free Travel

Citizens of certain countries are granted visa-free entry to French Polynesia, allowing them to visit Bora Bora for short stays without a visa. However, it is crucial to verify your country's visa exemption status and the maximum allowable duration of stay.

Visa on Arrival

For citizens of countries that are not visa-exempt, but have established visa-on-arrival agreements with French Polynesia, you can obtain a visa upon arrival at the port of entry in Bora Bora. This visa typically allows for a short stay for tourism purposes.

Tourist Visa

If your country does not qualify for visa-free travel or visa on arrival, you will need to apply for a tourist visa at the French embassy or consulate in your home country before your trip. The tourist visa will specify the duration of your stay and the purpose of your visit.

Business Visa

Travelers intending to conduct business activities in Bora Bora, such as attending conferences, meetings, or negotiating contracts, will require a business visa. This visa type may have specific requirements, so it's essential to check with the relevant authorities.

Transit Visa

If you are transiting through Bora Bora to another destination and have a layover exceeding a certain duration, you may need a transit visa. The transit visa allows you to stay in the country for a limited period while you wait for your onward flight.

Visa Application Process

The visa application process typically involves the following steps:

Online Application

Some countries offer an online visa application system, making the process more convenient and accessible. The online application platform provides guidance on required documents and processing fees.

Paper Application

If your country does not offer an online application option, you may need to submit a paper visa application at the nearest French embassy or consulate. In such cases, plan ahead and allow sufficient time for processing.

Supporting Documents

Visa applications require certain supporting documents, such as a valid passport, passport-size photographs, travel itinerary, proof of accommodation in Bora Bora, proof of sufficient funds for your stay, and an invitation letter (for business visas).

Processing Time

The processing time for visa applications varies depending on the country and the type of visa requested. It is advisable to apply well in advance of your travel date to account for any potential delays.

Visa Exemptions and Visa Waiver Programs

Some travelers may be eligible for visa exemptions or participate in visa waiver programs based on bilateral agreements or regional arrangements. Common examples include diplomatic passport holders, citizens of regional organizations, or participants in specific cultural exchange programs.

Entry and Exit Stamps

Upon arrival in Bora Bora, immigration officials will stamp your passport, indicating the date of entry. Likewise, when you leave the country, they will stamp your passport again with the date of departure. These entry and exit stamps are essential for monitoring your duration of stay and compliance with visa regulations.

Overstaying and Visa Extensions

It is crucial to abide by the authorized duration of stay specified on your visa or visa exemption. Overstaying can lead to penalties, fines, deportation, or difficulties with future travel to Bora Bora or other countries. If you need to extend your stay for legitimate reasons, contact the local immigration authorities to explore the possibility of a visa extension.

Dual Citizenship and Residency Permits

If you hold dual citizenship, make sure to use the same passport you used during the visa application process. Additionally, if you plan to reside in Bora Bora for an extended period, you may need to apply for a residency permit to ensure compliance with local regulations.

Special Cases: Family and Group Travel

If you are traveling with family or as part of a group, ensure that each member meets the passport and visa requirements. If you have children traveling with you, check whether they require separate passports or if they can be included in their parents' passports.

Travel Tips and Final Thoughts

Before traveling to Bora Bora, always double-check the latest passport and visa requirements. Gather all necessary documents, plan your trip well in advance, and allow sufficient time for visa processing. Stay informed about any changes in visa regulations and be prepared for a fantastic and unforgettable experience in Bora Bora.

Vaccinations and Health Tips

While Bora Bora offers a wealth of natural wonders and thrilling activities, it is essential for visitors to prioritize their health and well-being during their stay.

1: Understanding the Vaccination Landscape

1.1 Importance of Vaccinations: Vaccinations play a pivotal role in safeguarding travelers from infectious diseases prevalent in their destination. For Bora Bora, immunizations can provide protection against specific diseases and minimize the risk of contracting them during your stay.

1.2 Required and Recommended Vaccinations: Before visiting Bora Bora, it is essential to check the specific vaccination requirements and recommendations of your home country and the World Health Organization (WHO). Routine vaccinations, such as measles, mumps, rubella, diphtheria, tetanus, and pertussis, are typically recommended for all travelers. Additionally, vaccines for hepatitis A and typhoid are often recommended, as they can be contracted through contaminated food and water.

1.3 Yellow Fever: Bora Bora does not require a yellow fever vaccination for entry. However, travelers coming from countries with a risk of yellow fever transmission may need a certificate of vaccination to enter Bora Bora. It is crucial to check the latest requirements and updates from official sources.

2: Pre-Trip Health Preparations

2.1 Medical Check-Up: Before traveling to Bora Bora, schedule a visit to your healthcare provider for a thorough medical check-up. Inform them about your travel plans, and they can advise you on any necessary vaccinations and ensure you are in good health for your trip.

2.2 Allow Sufficient Time for Vaccinations: Some vaccinations require multiple doses over an extended period to provide full immunity. Plan ahead and give yourself ample time to complete the required vaccination schedule.

2.3 Stay Informed about Local Health Risks: Stay updated on any potential health risks in Bora Bora by checking with reputable sources such as the Centers for Disease Control and Prevention (CDC) or the WHO. Information about disease outbreaks or health alerts will help you make informed decisions while traveling.

3: Health Tips for Bora Bora Visitors

3.1 Hydration: The tropical climate of Bora Bora can be hot and humid, leading to an increased risk of dehydration. Drink plenty of bottled water throughout the day to stay hydrated, especially if engaging in outdoor activities.

3.2 Sun Protection: The sun's rays can be intense in Bora Bora, so it's crucial to protect your skin and eyes. Wear a broad-spectrum sunscreen with a high SPF, wide-brimmed hats, and sunglasses to shield yourself from harmful UV rays.

3.3 Insect Protection: Mosquito-borne illnesses, such as dengue fever and Zika virus, are present in some regions of the South Pacific, including French Polynesia. Use insect repellents containing DEET, wear long sleeves and pants during peak mosquito activity hours, and sleep under mosquito nets if needed.

3.4 Food and Water Safety: While Bora Bora is known for its delectable cuisine, practice caution when consuming street food or eating at local establishments. Stick to bottled water and avoid ice in drinks to reduce the risk of waterborne illnesses.

3.5 Motion Sickness: If you plan on taking boat rides or engaging in water activities, motion sickness can be a concern. Consider over-the-counter medications or natural remedies to prevent or alleviate motion sickness symptoms.

3.6 Respect Marine Life: Bora Bora's aquatic wonders attract visitors seeking snorkeling and diving adventures. Respect marine life and coral reefs by not touching or damaging them, and avoid purchasing souvenirs made from endangered species or coral.

4: Seek Medical Care If Needed

4.1 Recognize the Signs of Illness: It is crucial to recognize the early signs of illness and seek medical attention promptly if needed. Common symptoms such as fever, severe diarrhea, persistent vomiting, or unusual rashes should not be ignored.

4.2 Medical Facilities in Bora Bora: Bora Bora has medical facilities and clinics, but for serious or complex medical issues, patients may need to be transferred to Tahiti for advanced care. Consider purchasing travel insurance that covers medical evacuation if necessary.

How to Get to Bora Bora

1. Transportation Options to Bora Bora

1.1. International Flights

The primary gateway to Bora Bora is Fa'a'ā International Airport (PPT) located in Tahiti, French Polynesia. Travelers from around the world can find international flights that connect to PPT. Several major airlines offer flights to Tahiti, including Air Tahiti Nui, Air France, United Airlines, and Qantas.

1.2. Inter-island Flights

From Tahiti, visitors can book domestic flights to Bora Bora's Bora Bora Airport (BOB). Air Tahiti, the domestic airline, provides regular flights between Tahiti and Bora Bora. The flight duration is approximately 45 minutes and offers breathtaking views of the South Pacific.

1.3. Cruise Ships

Another popular way to reach Bora Bora is by cruise ships that operate in the region. Many cruise lines offer itineraries that include Bora Bora as one of the stops. This option allows travelers to explore multiple destinations in French Polynesia and experience the beauty of the South Pacific during the journey.

CHAPTER TWO:ACCOMMODATION OPTIONS

Luxury Resorts and Overwater Bungalows

The Allure of Bora Bora

Bora Bora is part of French Polynesia and is situated approximately 230 kilometers (143 miles) northwest of Tahiti. Its remote location in the middle of the Pacific Ocean adds to its exclusivity and allure. The island is surrounded by a vibrant coral reef, creating a barrier that protects the crystal-clear lagoon from the open ocean. This natural wonder provides opportunities for various water-based activities such as snorkeling, scuba diving, and swimming, making Bora Bora a haven for aquatic enthusiasts.

The island's lush landscapes, including the dormant volcano Mount Otemanu, add to its breathtaking beauty. The blend of stunning marine life and picturesque panoramas creates an idyllic setting that attracts couples seeking a romantic getaway, honeymooners in search of an unforgettable start to their married life, and travelers yearning for a serene escape from the hustle and bustle of daily life.

Evolution of Hospitality Industry

The history of Bora Bora's hospitality industry can be traced back to the 1960s when the island began to open up to tourism. Initially, basic lodgings were offered to visitors, but as the island's popularity grew, so did the demand for upscale accommodations. Recognizing the potential of Bora Bora as a high-end tourist destination, visionary entrepreneurs and international hotel chains started investing in luxury resorts on the island.

Over the years, Bora Bora's hospitality landscape evolved significantly, and it quickly became synonymous with opulence and exclusivity. Luxury resorts began to spring up along the coastline, offering guests an unparalleled experience of indulgence and relaxation. Today, Bora Bora boasts a plethora of high-end resorts, each vying to offer the most lavish amenities and experiences to their discerning clientele.

The Allure of Overwater Bungalows

One of the key attractions that set Bora Bora apart from other luxury destinations is its iconic overwater bungalows. The concept of overwater accommodations can be traced back to the 1960s when the first humble stilted bungalows were constructed above the lagoon. These simple structures captured the imagination of travelers, and overwater bungalows soon became synonymous with luxury and romance.

The allure of staying in an overwater bungalow is multifaceted. Firstly, the direct connection with the lagoon allows guests to immerse themselves in the captivating marine ecosystem right from their doorstep. Snorkeling in the crystal-clear waters and observing the vibrant marine life becomes an everyday delight. Secondly, the unobstructed views of the turquoise lagoon and the majestic Mount Otemanu in the background create an ethereal atmosphere, perfect for relaxation and introspection.

Moreover, the privacy and seclusion provided by overwater bungalows appeal to high-profile individuals, celebrities, and honeymooners seeking an exclusive escape from the public eye. The feeling of being suspended above the water, surrounded by nothing but the soothing sounds of the ocean, is an experience that remains etched in the memories of visitors for a lifetime.

Luxury Resorts and Their Offerings

Bora Bora's luxury resorts are renowned for their world-class services, attention to detail, and the fusion of modern comforts with traditional Polynesian charm. Each resort strives to outdo the others by offering a wide array of amenities and activities that cater to the unique preferences of their guests.

1. Overwater Bungalows with Private Plunge Pools: Many luxury resorts in Bora Bora have taken opulence to new heights by introducing overwater bungalows equipped with private plunge pools. These pools provide an exclusive and intimate space for guests to unwind and soak in the awe-inspiring vistas surrounding them.

2. Gourmet Dining Experience: The resorts on the island boast exquisite dining options, with some featuring world-renowned chefs who curate exceptional menus. Guests can indulge in a diverse range of international and local delicacies, often served in romantic settings like private beachside cabanas or on a deck above the lagoon.

3. Spa and Wellness Retreats: Bora Bora's luxury resorts are home to state-of-the-art spa and wellness facilities. Guests can indulge in various rejuvenating treatments, including traditional Polynesian massages and therapies, to soothe both body and soul.

4. Water-Based Activities: Resorts offer an abundance of water-based activities such as paddleboarding, jet skiing, and sailing. Additionally, many resorts have their private stretches of beach, where guests can relax under the warm tropical sun or engage in beach volleyball and other sports.

5. Romantic Experiences: As a favored destination for honeymooners and couples celebrating special occasions, Bora Bora's resorts offer an array of romantic experiences. From private candlelit dinners on the beach to couples' massages and stargazing excursions, every detail is tailored to create cherished memories.

Environmental Sustainability

While the allure of luxury and opulence may be the primary draw for visitors, the hospitality industry in Bora Bora has also recognized the importance of environmental sustainability. Efforts have been made to preserve the pristine natural beauty of the island and the delicate marine ecosystem that surrounds it.

Many resorts have implemented eco-friendly practices, such as waste reduction, water conservation, and the use of renewable energy sources. Some resorts actively participate in coral restoration programs to protect the reef, ensuring that future generations can continue to experience the enchanting underwater world.

Mid-Range Hotels and Beachfront Villas

Mid-Range Hotels

1. Hotel Maitai Bora Bora

Situated on the main island of Bora Bora, Hotel Maitai Bora Bora offers a comfortable and affordable mid-range option for visitors. The hotel's bungalows are nestled amidst lush gardens or along the beach, providing guests with a serene atmosphere and beautiful views. While not as luxurious as the high-end resorts, Hotel Maitai compensates with its friendly staff and authentic Polynesian charm.

Amenities: The hotel offers various amenities, including an on-site restaurant serving local and international cuisine, a beach bar for refreshing tropical drinks, water sports facilities, and organized excursions such as snorkeling and lagoon tours.

Location: Matira Point, the hotel's location, is renowned for its stunning sunsets and is within walking distance of Matira Beach, one of the most picturesque beaches on the island.

2. Sofitel Bora Bora Marara Beach Resort

For visitors seeking a touch of luxury without breaking the bank, Sofitel Bora Bora Marara Beach Resort is an excellent mid-range option. The resort combines Polynesian style with modern comforts, making it an attractive choice for couples and families alike.

Amenities: Sofitel Bora Bora Marara offers a range of amenities, including a beautiful infinity pool overlooking the lagoon, a spa offering relaxing treatments, and multiple dining options serving French, Polynesian, and international cuisine.

Location: The resort is located on the mainland, conveniently close to the main town of Vaitape, where visitors can explore local markets and experience the island's vibrant culture.

3. InterContinental Le Moana Bora Bora

InterContinental Le Moana is another mid-range hotel option, situated on the southern tip of the main island. The resort boasts a relaxed and intimate ambiance, making it an ideal choice for honeymooners and couples seeking a romantic escape.

Amenities: Guests can enjoy a private beach, a beachside restaurant serving delectable seafood, and spacious overwater bungalows with direct access to the crystal-clear lagoon.

Location: The hotel's location provides easy access to some of Bora Bora's best snorkeling spots, where visitors can encounter vibrant marine life and colorful coral reefs.

Beachfront Villas

1. Four Seasons Resort Bora Bora

For those looking for a lavish and exclusive beachfront experience, the Four Seasons Resort in Bora Bora is an unparalleled choice. The resort is synonymous with luxury and has consistently been ranked as one of the world's best beachfront properties.

Amenities: The Four Seasons offers an array of top-notch amenities, including spacious overwater bungalows with private plunge pools, a world-class spa, fine dining restaurants, and personalized services.

Location: Located on a private motu (small islet), the resort provides a secluded and tranquil environment, surrounded by the mesmerizing waters of the lagoon.

2. St. Regis Bora Bora Resort

The St. Regis Bora Bora Resort epitomizes sophistication and elegance, promising an unforgettable stay in one of the most luxurious settings in the world. The resort's iconic overwater bungalows and private villas create a haven of opulence and comfort.

Amenities: The resort offers an impressive list of amenities, including the Miri Miri Spa by Clarins, a lagoon-view restaurant with exquisite cuisine, and personalized services like butler assistance.

Location: Nestled on the secluded northeastern side of the lagoon, the St. Regis Resort boasts breathtaking views of Mount Otemanu and the turquoise waters that surround it.

3. Conrad Bora Bora Nui

Conrad Bora Bora Nui is a stunning beachfront property that promises an extraordinary escape in paradise. With its contemporary design and lavish facilities, the resort caters to discerning travelers seeking a refined and indulgent experience.

Amenities: The resort boasts an array of luxurious amenities, including overwater villas with glass floors, a hilltop spa offering panoramic views, multiple dining options, and a plethora of water-based activities.

Location: Conrad Bora Bora Nui is located on a motu, providing guests with a sense of seclusion and tranquility, while still being within reach of the mainland's attractions.

Budget-Friendly Lodging

Bora Bora, with its stunning turquoise waters, lush greenery, and overwater bungalows, is undoubtedly a dream destination for many travelers. However, the allure of this picturesque island often comes with a perception of high costs. While it is true that Bora Bora can be an expensive destination, there are budget-friendly lodging options available for visitors who wish to experience this paradise without breaking the bank.

1.Choosing Budget-Friendly Accommodations:

a) Guesthouses and Pension Houses: One of the best ways to save on accommodation in Bora Bora is by opting for guesthouses or pension houses. These are smaller, family-run establishments that offer more affordable rates compared to luxury resorts. While they may lack some of the opulent amenities of larger resorts, guesthouses provide a more authentic local experience and often have breathtaking views.

b) Camping: For the adventurous and budget-conscious traveler, camping is an option worth considering. Bora Bora has some designated camping areas, and staying in a tent can significantly reduce accommodation expenses. However, do check the local regulations and get proper permits before planning a camping trip.

c) Shared Accommodations: With the rise of platforms like Airbnb, it has become easier to find shared accommodations or private rooms in local residences. This option can be more cost-effective than booking a full-fledged resort, especially for solo travelers or couples.

2. Traveling During Off-Peak Seasons:

Bora Bora's high season typically runs from May to October when the weather is cooler and drier. During this time, the island experiences an influx of tourists, and prices for accommodation and activities are at their highest. Traveling during the shoulder or off-peak seasons (November to April) can result in significant cost savings.

3. Booking In Advance:

Regardless of the type of accommodation you choose, booking well in advance is an excellent way to secure better deals. As demand for lodging can be high, especially during peak seasons, early bookings often come with discounts.

4. All-Inclusive Packages:

While all-inclusive resorts can be pricey, they may still offer good value for money for some travelers. All-inclusive packages typically include meals, drinks, activities, and sometimes even airfare. If you plan to make use of various activities and services offered by the resort, these packages might be worth considering to avoid unexpected expenses.

5. Self-Catering Options:

If your accommodation includes a kitchenette or a shared kitchen, consider preparing some of your meals. Buying groceries from local markets and supermarkets can be more cost-effective than dining out for every meal.

6. Exploring Local Cuisine:

Sampling the local cuisine is a must when visiting any destination, and Bora Bora is no exception. However, dining in high-end restaurants can quickly add up. To save on food costs, try out local food trucks, small eateries, and market stalls. Not only will you save money, but you'll also get a taste of authentic Polynesian dishes.

7. Free and Low-Cost Activities:

Bora Bora offers a wealth of natural beauty and activities that won't cost you a fortune. Enjoy the island's pristine beaches, go hiking or cycling, and take advantage of free water activities like snorkeling in the crystal-clear lagoons. Exploring the island's lush landscapes and interacting with local culture are rewarding experiences that come without a hefty price tag.

8. Group Activities and Excursions:

Consider joining group activities and excursions as they can often be more economical than private tours. Many tour operators offer various packages, from snorkeling tours to shark and ray feeding experiences. Group rates can be more budget-friendly and also offer the opportunity to meet other travelers.

9. Using Public Transportation:

While Bora Bora is relatively small, getting around can be expensive if you rely solely on taxis. Instead, use the island's public transportation system, which usually involves small buses, to travel between the main points of interest.

10. Setting a Realistic Budget:

Before embarking on your Bora Bora adventure, set a budget for your trip and stick to it. Track your expenses and be mindful of your spending. Having a clear budget in mind will help you make more informed decisions and ensure you don't overspend.

CHAPTER THREE:EXPLORING BORA BORA

Top Attractions and Landmarks

Mount Otemanu: Standing majestically at 2,385 feet (727 meters) above sea level, Mount Otemanu is the highest peak in Bora Bora and an iconic landmark on the island. This dormant volcano offers breathtaking views of the entire island and its surrounding lagoon. While the climb to the summit is challenging and requires a guide, the panoramic vistas make it well worth the effort for adventurous travelers.

Bora Bora Lagoonarium: The Bora Bora Lagoonarium is a unique and family-friendly attraction where visitors can get up close and personal with a variety of marine life. Snorkeling and swimming in the crystal-clear waters of the lagoon, visitors can encounter friendly stingrays, sharks, and colorful tropical fish. This immersive experience provides a deeper appreciation for the island's stunning marine ecosystem.

Matira Beach: Regarded as one of the most beautiful beaches in the world, Matira Beach is a must-visit destination in Bora Bora. With its fine white sand and gentle turquoise waters, the beach offers an ideal spot for swimming, sunbathing, and romantic sunset strolls. Numerous beachside bars and restaurants serve delectable Polynesian cuisine, adding to the beach's allure.

Coral Gardens: For snorkeling enthusiasts, Coral Gardens is an underwater paradise showcasing an array of coral formations and marine life. Situated within the Bora Bora lagoon, this protected area boasts a vibrant underwater ecosystem that includes colorful coral reefs, tropical fish, and even occasional visits from gentle manta rays and eagle rays.

Matira Point: Located at the southern end of Matira Beach, Matira Point is a picturesque peninsula that offers stunning views of the lagoon and Mount Otemanu. The area is a popular spot for picnicking and relaxation, as well as a great vantage point for observing local outrigger canoes gliding across the calm waters.

Bora Bora Turtle Center: Founded in 2004, the Bora Bora Turtle Center is a conservation facility dedicated to rehabilitating and protecting endangered sea turtles. Visitors can learn about the various species of turtles found in the South Pacific, their life cycles, and the center's efforts to conserve these magnificent creatures. This is a rewarding and educational experience for visitors of all ages.

Vaitape: As the main village and commercial hub of Bora Bora, Vaitape offers a glimpse into the local way of life. Visitors can explore charming boutiques, art galleries, and craft shops, where they can purchase unique souvenirs and handicrafts created by local artisans. The town's open-air market is a great place to savor the island's fresh produce and interact with friendly locals.

Bloody Mary's Restaurant & Bar: No visit to Bora Bora is complete without dining at the iconic Bloody Mary's Restaurant & Bar. Frequented by celebrities and travelers alike, this legendary establishment offers a laid-back atmosphere and a delectable menu featuring seafood and Polynesian-inspired dishes. Visitors can also leave their mark by etching their names onto the restaurant's sand floor.

Motu Tapu: Situated just off the coast of Bora Bora, Motu Tapu is a private islet renowned for its pristine beaches, swaying palm trees, and exclusive resorts. Many all-inclusive resorts offer day trips and excursions to this secluded paradise, where visitors can bask in the sun, indulge in water sports, and enjoy a private picnic on the beach.

Faanui Bay: For those seeking a more authentic experience, Faanui Bay provides an opportunity to observe the local lifestyle and fishing traditions of Bora Bora. Visitors can take guided boat tours through the bay, interact with friendly fishermen, and even learn about traditional Polynesian fishing techniques.

Amanahune Bay: Amanahune Bay is a serene and less-visited area in Bora Bora, making it perfect for travelers seeking tranquility and seclusion. The bay is dotted with small motus (islets) and offers excellent snorkeling opportunities. Many boat tours include stops at Amanahune Bay, allowing visitors to explore its untouched beauty.

Anau: Anau is a charming village on Bora Bora that provides a glimpse into the local culture and daily life of the island's inhabitants. Visitors can wander through the village's lush gardens, visit a vanilla plantation, and interact with friendly locals, gaining insight into their customs and traditions.

Mount Pahia and Mount Ohue: For hikers and adventurers, Mount Pahia and Mount Ohue offer thrilling and challenging experiences. These peaks, located in the heart of Bora Bora, provide a chance to explore the island's rugged interior and lush vegetation. Guided tours are recommended for safety and to fully appreciate the natural beauty of the surroundings.

Motu Tapuaetai (One Foot Island): While Motu Tapu is a private island, Motu Tapuaetai, also known as One Foot Island, is open to the public and offers visitors a slice of paradise. Famous for its stunning sandbars and crystal-clear waters, this small islet is a popular spot for snorkeling and beachcombing. Many tour operators offer day trips to Motu Tapuaetai, providing an unforgettable experience.

Bora Bora Helicopter Tours: For a truly awe-inspiring experience, visitors can opt for a helicopter tour to witness Bora Bora's beauty from the sky. These tours offer stunning aerial views of the island's lagoon, coral reefs, and volcanic peaks, creating memories that will last a lifetime.

Matira Beach - The Jewel of Bora Bora

Historical Background:

Before we immerse ourselves in the contemporary beauty of Matira Beach, it is essential to grasp its historical significance. The origins of Bora Bora date back to the Polynesian migration, where intrepid seafarers first settled on the island over a thousand years ago. The name "Bora Bora" is thought to stem from the Tahitian language, with "Bora" meaning "first born" and "Pora Pora" signifying "created by the gods."

Over the centuries, the island was visited by European explorers like Captain James Cook in the 18th century, leading to its inclusion in the French colonial empire. The region's tranquil charm and captivating beauty started attracting tourists in the early 20th century, eventually establishing Bora Bora as a prominent tourist destination, with Matira Beach at its heart.

Geographical Features:

Matira Beach stretches for about one mile along the southern tip of Bora Bora. It boasts a unique geographical layout, where the beach is backed by lush vegetation and dense coconut groves, providing a natural barrier between the sands and the rest of the island. The beach's northwestern orientation ensures it benefits from breathtaking sunsets, making it a prime spot for romantic getaways.

The pristine waters of Matira Beach are protected by a vibrant coral reef, creating a tranquil lagoon that allows for safe swimming and snorkeling. The coral reef also plays a crucial role in preserving the marine ecosystem, home to an array of colorful fish and other aquatic creatures.

Activities and Recreation:

For adventure seekers and leisure travelers alike, Matira Beach offers a plethora of activities and recreational opportunities to satisfy every desire.

a. Water Sports: The calm waters of the lagoon are perfect for a variety of water sports such as snorkeling, paddleboarding, kayaking, and jet-skiing. Snorkeling in the coral gardens allows visitors to explore the mesmerizing underwater world, encountering vibrant coral formations and an abundance of marine life.

b. Diving: Scuba diving enthusiasts are in for a treat as Bora Bora's surrounding waters offer a diverse range of dive sites, including underwater caves, shipwrecks, and encounters with graceful manta rays and gentle sharks.

c. Romantic Sunset Cruises: Couples can indulge in a romantic sunset cruise on traditional Polynesian outrigger canoes, savoring the breathtaking beauty of the setting sun against the backdrop of the island's lush landscape.

d. Island Tours: Guided tours of Bora Bora offer insight into the island's rich cultural heritage and showcase the warmth and hospitality of its people. Tourists can visit ancient temples, learn about traditional crafts, and experience the vibrant local life.

e. Helicopter Tours: For a truly unforgettable experience, visitors can take to the skies on a helicopter tour, providing a bird's-eye view of the island's mesmerizing beauty, including the iconic Mount Otemanu and the vibrant turquoise lagoon.

f. Relaxation and Beachcombing: Of course, no visit to Matira Beach would be complete without simply basking in the sun, lounging under the shade of palm trees, and strolling along the soft sands while collecting seashells and enjoying the gentle ocean breeze.

Accommodations:

Bora Bora boasts a range of luxurious resorts and overwater bungalows, many of which are situated along the shores of Matira Beach. These accommodations cater to every indulgence and provide unparalleled views of the azure lagoon and surrounding landscapes. Visitors can choose from elegant resorts that offer private bungalows with direct access to the water, ensuring a truly immersive island experience.

The overwater bungalows are especially popular and have become an iconic symbol of Bora Bora. They offer a sense of serenity and luxury, with guests waking up to the soothing sounds of lapping waves beneath their floorboards and the opportunity to take a refreshing dip straight from their private decks.

Cultural Highlights:

Bora Bora, like the rest of French Polynesia, is steeped in cultural richness and heritage. The local Tahitian culture is celebrated through traditional dance, music, and crafts. Visitors can immerse themselves in the island's customs and traditions by attending local performances, visiting artisanal markets, and partaking in authentic Polynesian cuisine.

Tahitian dance, known as 'Ori Tahiti', is a vibrant and captivating art form that tells stories through rhythmic movements and expressive gestures. It is often performed at hotels and cultural centers for tourists to experience the depth of the island's cultural roots.

Environmental Conservation:

As the popularity of Matira Beach and Bora Bora as a whole continues to grow, there is an increasing focus on environmental conservation to protect this precious ecosystem. Efforts are made to minimize the impact of tourism on the coral reefs, marine life, and native flora and fauna. Many resorts promote eco-friendly practices and educate visitors about the importance of preserving the natural beauty of the island for future generations.

Mount Otemanu - A Majestic Peak

The Geological Marvel:

Mount Otemanu is the highest peak on the island of Bora Bora, which is a part of the Society Islands archipelago in French Polynesia. The island itself is a product of volcanic activity that occurred over millions of years, and Mount Otemanu represents the remnants of one of these ancient volcanoes. Geologically classified as a stratovolcano, it is characterized by steep slopes and a distinctive cone shape, making it an impressive sight even from afar.

Visitors are often fascinated by the dramatic formation of the mountain, which is adorned with lush greenery and sheer rock faces. As the central landmark of Bora Bora, Mount Otemanu is visible from various vantage points on the island, and its magnetic allure draws in adventurers and nature enthusiasts alike.

Cultural Significance:

For the local Tahitian people, Mount Otemanu holds deep cultural significance and is steeped in legends and myths. It is considered a sacred site, believed to be the dwelling place of their gods and a source of spiritual energy. The ancient Tahitians worshiped and respected the mountain, attributing it with mystical powers that helped shape their beliefs and traditions.

Visitors exploring Mount Otemanu may encounter local guides and storytellers who are eager to share the island's cultural heritage. Hearing the tales of the Tahitian people and understanding their connection to this majestic peak adds an enriching layer to the overall experience.

Trekking and Hiking:

For adventurers seeking an adrenaline-pumping experience, Mount Otemanu offers fantastic hiking and trekking opportunities. While the ascent is challenging and only suitable for experienced hikers, the rewards are unparalleled. The trek to the summit is a journey through diverse landscapes, from tropical forests to rocky terrains, offering breathtaking vistas at every turn.

Hiking routes are well-marked, and guided tours are available for those who prefer to have expert knowledge and support. The trek usually takes several hours to complete, and it's recommended to start early in the day to avoid the heat and ensure a safer climb.

Aerial Views:

One of the most spectacular ways to appreciate the grandeur of Mount Otemanu is from the sky. Helicopter tours and scenic flights are popular options for visitors who want to take in the panoramic views of the entire island, with the imposing peak as the centerpiece.

Flying over the crystal-clear lagoon, coral reefs, and luxurious overwater bungalows, you'll gain a new perspective on the island's beauty. The aerial tour also provides an excellent opportunity to capture stunning photographs of the landscape and create lasting memories of Bora Bora's natural splendor.

Diving and Snorkeling:

The allure of Bora Bora extends underwater, where a vibrant marine ecosystem awaits exploration. The lagoon surrounding the island is a sanctuary for marine life, offering diverse coral reefs and an abundance of colorful fish.

Snorkeling and diving around Mount Otemanu provide a unique experience, as the underwater terrain features lava tubes and caves formed by volcanic activity. The waters are teeming with marine life, including rays, sharks, and various tropical fish species. Exploring the aquatic wonderland against the backdrop of the majestic mountain is an unforgettable adventure for water enthusiasts.

Sunset Magic:

As the day draws to a close, Mount Otemanu takes on a new splendor during sunset. The changing hues of the sky cast a golden glow upon the mountain, creating a magical atmosphere that enchants visitors and locals alike.

Many resorts offer sunset cruises or catamaran tours, providing an opportunity to witness this awe-inspiring spectacle from the water. Couples looking for a romantic experience can enjoy a private dinner on the beach, with the silhouetted Mount Otemanu adding an unforgettable backdrop to their evening.

Accommodation:

Several luxury resorts on Bora Bora offer exclusive views of Mount Otemanu, allowing guests to wake up to the sight of the magnificent peak each morning. Overwater bungalows and beachfront villas provide the perfect balance of comfort and natural beauty.

Staying in such accommodations ensures that visitors have easy access to the island's main attraction and can relish the serenity of the surroundings. The resorts often arrange special experiences and activities, including guided hikes, water sports, and cultural tours, making it a seamless way to enjoy everything Mount Otemanu and Bora Bora have to offer.

Bora Bora Lagoonarium - A Marine Wonderland

The Enchanting History of Bora Bora Lagoonarium

The Bora Bora Lagoonarium has a rich history that dates back centuries. The island of Bora Bora itself has been inhabited by Polynesians since ancient times, and they have always had a close connection to the surrounding lagoon and its marine life. The concept of the lagoonarium emerged in the mid-20th century when the island's inhabitants sought to create a protected environment where visitors could interact with the diverse marine species found in the lagoon without disturbing the delicate ecosystem.

The idea was brought to fruition by a group of visionary locals who collaborated with marine biologists and conservationists. They worked hand in hand to ensure the lagoonarium's design and practices adhered to sustainable and responsible tourism principles. Through their efforts, the Bora

Bora Lagoonarium opened its doors to visitors, providing them with a once-in-a-lifetime opportunity to experience the wonders of the underwater world in a safe and respectful manner.

Immersive Attractions and Activities

Snorkeling: Undoubtedly, snorkeling is the highlight of any visit to the Bora Bora Lagoonarium. The pristine waters of the lagoon are teeming with an incredible array of marine life, including colorful fish, rays, sharks, and even turtles. Snorkelers can swim alongside these gentle creatures and witness their natural behaviors up close, creating memories that will last a lifetime.

Guided Tours: For those who prefer a more educational experience, the lagoonarium offers guided tours led by marine experts. These experts share their extensive knowledge about the marine ecosystem, the species that call the lagoon home, and the conservation efforts in place to protect them. Visitors will leave with a deeper understanding and appreciation for the delicate balance of life within the lagoon.

Fish Feeding Shows: One of the most delightful spectacles at the lagoonarium is the fish feeding shows. During these events, visitors have the opportunity to watch as experienced handlers feed the fish and interact with them. It's a thrilling sight to see the colorful fish swarming around, creating a breathtaking display of nature's wonders.

Shark and Ray Interaction: For the more adventurous souls, the lagoonarium offers the chance to swim alongside harmless blacktip reef sharks and rays. These graceful creatures are accustomed to human presence and are incredibly docile. Under the watchful eye of trained professionals, visitors can experience the thrill of being in such close proximity to these fascinating animals.

Beachside Relaxation: The lagoonarium isn't just about aquatic adventures; it also offers a tranquil beach where visitors can unwind and soak in the beauty of their surroundings. Sunbathing, beachcombing, and simply enjoying the stunning scenery are popular activities for those seeking a more laid-back experience.

Conservation and Sustainable Practices

The Bora Bora Lagoonarium takes its responsibility as a guardian of the marine ecosystem very seriously. Conservation efforts are at the heart of everything they do, ensuring that the delicate balance of the lagoon's biodiversity remains undisturbed for generations to come. Some of the initiatives in place include:

Education and Awareness: The lagoonarium actively participates in educational programs for locals and visitors alike. They believe that by fostering a deeper understanding and appreciation for marine life, they can inspire a sense of stewardship and responsibility towards the environment.

No Feeding of Wildlife: To maintain the natural behaviors and health of the marine species, the lagoonarium strictly prohibits visitors from feeding the fish, sharks, and rays. This ensures that the animals' diet remains natural and balanced, preventing potential harm to their health and the ecosystem.

Limited Daily Capacity: The lagoonarium carefully manages the number of visitors allowed each day to avoid overcrowding and undue stress on marine life. By controlling the number of people in the lagoon, they can maintain a serene and harmonious environment for both visitors and animals.

Sustainable Infrastructure: The facilities and structures within the lagoonarium are designed to have minimal impact on the surrounding environment. Great care is taken in waste management, energy usage, and water conservation practices.

Supporting Research: The lagoonarium actively collaborates with marine biologists and researchers to contribute valuable data and insights into the region's marine ecology. This research aids in the development of effective conservation strategies and policies.

Practical Information for Visitors

Best Time to Visit: Bora Bora is a year-round destination, but the peak tourist season generally falls between May and October when the weather is drier and cooler. However, this also means larger crowds and higher prices. If you prefer a quieter experience, consider visiting during the shoulder seasons.

Getting There: The island of Bora Bora is accessible by air and sea. Visitors usually arrive at Fa'a'ā International Airport in Papeete, Tahiti, and then take a short domestic flight to Bora Bora Airport. Alternatively, cruise ships also dock at Bora Bora, offering a scenic approach to the island.

Accommodation: Bora Bora offers a range of accommodation options, including luxurious overwater bungalows and charming beachfront resorts. It is advisable to book accommodation well in advance, especially during peak seasons.

Lagoonarium Entry: To experience the wonders of the Bora Bora Lagoonarium, visitors can purchase tickets on-site or through authorized tour operators. The entry fee typically covers the guided tour and snorkeling activities.

What to Bring: Remember to pack essentials such as sunscreen, swimwear, a hat, and a waterproof camera to capture the mesmerizing underwater world. Snorkeling gear is often provided on-site, but you may prefer to bring your own for comfort and hygiene.

Coral Gardens - Snorkeling Haven

What are Coral Gardens?

Coral Gardens, also known as coral reefs or coral colonies, are vibrant underwater ecosystems created by colonies of tiny marine animals called polyps. These polyps produce calcium carbonate, forming hard skeletons that build up over time, forming the coral structures we see today. The combination of living coral polyps and the diverse marine life they attract makes coral gardens a vital part of marine biodiversity.

The Magnificent Beauty of Bora Bora's Coral Gardens

Bora Bora's Coral Gardens stand out for their unparalleled beauty and diversity. The island is surrounded by a lagoon teeming with colorful corals and an abundance of marine species. The coral gardens come alive with a kaleidoscope of colors, ranging from vibrant reds and pinks to blues, purples, and yellows. Visitors can explore the lagoon's shallow waters, providing a unique opportunity to observe this captivating marine ecosystem up close.

Ecological Importance of Coral Gardens

Coral gardens play a crucial role in maintaining marine biodiversity and supporting various marine species. They serve as breeding grounds and habitats for numerous fish, mollusks, crustaceans, and other marine creatures. Additionally, coral reefs act as natural barriers, protecting coastlines from erosion, storms, and strong ocean currents.

Bora Bora's Coral Gardens contribute significantly to the overall health of the Pacific Ocean ecosystem. By providing shelter and sustenance to marine life, they help maintain the delicate balance of the underwater environment. Furthermore, they contribute to the carbon and nutrient cycles, making them essential players in global ecological systems.

Snorkeling and Diving: The Ultimate Coral Garden Experience

For visitors, snorkeling and diving are the primary ways to experience the enchanting beauty of Bora Bora's Coral Gardens. Snorkeling allows individuals of all ages and skill levels to float on the surface of the water and observe the vibrant underwater world. The lagoon's shallow waters make it an ideal location for beginners to explore this natural wonder safely.

On the other hand, diving offers a more immersive experience for certified divers. Descending into the depths of the lagoon unveils a whole new world of marine life. Divers can get closer to the corals and interact with a more extensive range of marine species, including rays, sharks, and even the elusive humpback whales during certain seasons.

Coral Conservation Efforts

Despite their importance, coral gardens worldwide are facing significant threats due to human activities and climate change. Coral bleaching, caused by rising sea temperatures, pollution, and ocean acidification, poses a severe risk to the survival of these fragile ecosystems.

In Bora Bora, efforts to protect and conserve the Coral Gardens have gained momentum in recent years. Local authorities, environmental organizations, and businesses have come together to implement conservation programs, raise awareness, and educate visitors and residents about the importance of preserving this precious natural resource.

Measures such as implementing marine protected areas, establishing sustainable tourism practices, and promoting responsible snorkeling and diving are essential steps in safeguarding the future of Bora Bora's Coral Gardens.

Responsible Tourism and Coral Gardens

As the popularity of Bora Bora as a tourist destination increases, so does the potential impact on the Coral

Gardens. Responsible tourism is critical in ensuring that visitors can enjoy this natural wonder without causing harm to the environment.

Visitors are encouraged to follow guidelines set by local authorities and tour operators to protect the coral reefs. Avoiding physical contact with corals, not feeding marine life, and using eco-friendly sunscreens are just a few ways tourists can contribute positively to coral conservation.

CHAPTER FOUR:WATER ACTIVITIES

Snorkeling Spots and Tips

Snorkeling Spots in Bora Bora

Matira Beach: One of the most popular snorkeling spots on the island, Matira Beach, offers a calm and shallow lagoon teeming with colorful marine life. Beginners and experienced snorkelers can enjoy exploring the coral gardens, encountering various fish species like parrotfish, butterflyfish, and clownfish. The sandy bottom and gentle current make it a great spot for family snorkeling excursions.

Coral Gardens: Located on the east side of the island, the Coral Gardens boast an incredible diversity of coral formations and marine creatures. As you snorkel through the clear waters, you'll come across graceful rays, small sharks, and even sea turtles. The Coral Gardens are a must-visit for those looking to experience the full spectrum of Bora Bora's underwater beauty.

Anau: Offering a less crowded snorkeling experience, Anau is perfect for those seeking tranquility. The shallow lagoon is home to numerous coral bommies and schools of tropical fish. It's an ideal location to relax, take in the breathtaking views of Mount Otemanu in the background, and get up close and personal with friendly marine life.

Mind the Tides: Pay attention to the tide levels and currents before snorkeling. Some spots may have stronger currents at certain times, and it's essential to be aware of potential hazards.

Snorkel Safely with Marine Life: While snorkeling with marine life can be an awe-inspiring experience, maintain a safe distance and avoid disturbing them. Do not feed the fish or any other marine creatures, as it can disrupt their natural behavior.

Stay Informed about Weather Conditions: Keep an eye on weather forecasts and consult local experts before heading out for a snorkeling session. Unpredictable weather can impact water conditions and snorkeling safety.

Join Guided Tours: For those new to snorkeling or unfamiliar with the area, guided snorkeling tours offer expert guidance, safety, and valuable insights into the marine life of Bora Bora. Certified guides can also help you spot hidden gems and maximize your snorkeling experience.

Scuba Diving Adventures

Scuba Diving Sites:

Anau: Anau is a popular dive site located on the eastern side of Bora Bora. This site is perfect for divers of all levels due to its gentle currents and shallow depths. As you descend, you'll be greeted by a vibrant coral garden teeming with a kaleidoscope of tropical fish, including butterflyfish, angelfish, and parrotfish. Keep an eye out for shy reef sharks and graceful eagle rays gliding effortlessly through the water.

Tapu: Tapu, situated just off the southern tip of Bora Bora, is a thrilling drift dive that offers a chance to encounter larger marine life. Divers can witness gray reef sharks, lemon sharks, and blacktip sharks as they patrol the area. The abundance of colorful soft corals and sea fans creates a striking backdrop against the deep blue water, providing an unforgettable experience.

Muri Muri: Muri Muri is an advanced dive site located on the northern side of the island. This site features stunning underwater topography, including dramatic drop-offs, caves, and swim-throughs. Advanced divers will relish the opportunity to explore the depths and spot schools of barracuda, jackfish, and occasional manta rays passing by.

Teavana Pass: Teavana Pass is a unique drift dive that takes you through the pass on the western side of the island. This site is famous for its encounters with large pelagic species, such as eagle rays, humphead wrasses, and even the elusive hammerhead sharks if you're lucky. Be prepared for an adrenaline-pumping ride as you glide with the currents through the pass.

Toopua: Toopua is a shallow dive site with a maximum depth of about 40 feet (12 meters), making it perfect for beginner divers. The waters are home to gentle blacktip sharks, stingrays, and an array of coral formations. The easy conditions and abundant marine life make this a favorite site for underwater photography.

Scuba Diving Schools and Tours:

Bora Bora offers several reputable scuba diving schools and tour operators that cater to divers of all levels. These dive centers are staffed by experienced instructors who prioritize safety and conservation while ensuring an unforgettable experience.

Top Dive Bora Bora: Top Dive Bora Bora is one of the most well-established dive centers on the island, known for its professionalism and commitment to eco-friendly practices. They offer a range of dive packages, including beginners' courses, guided dives, and specialized excursions for experienced divers.

Diveasy Bora Bora: Diveasy Bora Bora is a PADI-certified dive center with a focus on personalized service. They offer small group dives, ensuring a more intimate and personalized experience for their guests. Diveasy also conducts regular coral conservation initiatives, giving visitors an opportunity to contribute positively to the marine ecosystem.

Bora Diving Center: Bora Diving Center is another reputable establishment that offers a wide range of dive options, from introductory dives to advanced excursions. Their experienced team of instructors provides thorough briefings and ensures that divers are well-prepared for each dive.

Marine Conservation Efforts:

As visitors, it is essential to appreciate the delicate balance of Bora Bora's marine ecosystem and participate in conservation efforts. Many scuba diving operators on the island are actively involved in marine conservation initiatives, such as coral reef restoration, ocean cleanups, and shark protection programs. By supporting these efforts, you can leave a positive impact on the environment and help preserve Bora Bora's underwater wonders for future generations.

Shark and Ray Feeding Excursions

The History and Significance of Shark and Ray Feeding Excursions in Bora Bora:

The tradition of shark and ray feeding excursions in Bora Bora dates back to the early 1980s when local fishermen discovered that sharks and rays were attracted to the sound of boat engines. They soon realized the potential for tourism and began offering guided tours, introducing visitors to these magnificent creatures while also providing an alternative source of income for the island's residents.

As word spread about the unique and thrilling experience of swimming with sharks and rays, Bora Bora quickly became a must-visit destination for adventure seekers and marine enthusiasts. Shark and ray feeding excursions not only allow visitors to witness these predators in their natural habitat but also contribute to the local economy and foster a deeper understanding and appreciation for marine life conservation efforts.

The Fascinating Marine Life of Bora Bora:

Bora Bora's crystal-clear lagoons are home to a diverse array of marine species, making it an ideal location for shark and ray feeding excursions. Some of the most common species encountered during these excursions include:

a) Blacktip Reef Sharks: These sleek and powerful predators are among the most common sharks found in Bora Bora's shallow waters. Known for their black-tipped fins, they are generally harmless to humans and prefer to feed on small fish and squid.

b) Lemon Sharks: Named for their yellowish-brown coloration, lemon sharks are often seen patrolling the lagoon's outer reef. Despite their formidable appearance, they are generally not aggressive towards humans and are essential components of the local marine ecosystem.

c) Stingrays: Bora Bora's shallow waters are also frequented by graceful stingrays. These gentle creatures are easily recognizable by their flat bodies and long, whip-like tails, which they use for protection and communication.

d) Manta Rays: Occasionally, lucky visitors may have the chance to encounter manta rays during their excursions. These majestic giants can grow up to 20 feet in wingspan, making for an awe-inspiring sight.

Eco-Tourism Initiatives and Conservation Efforts:

As the popularity of shark and ray feeding excursions has grown, so too has the awareness of the need to protect these fragile marine ecosystems. To ensure sustainable tourism practices and the preservation of Bora Bora's marine life, several eco-tourism initiatives have been implemented.

a) Responsible Feeding Practices: Tour operators now adhere to strict guidelines for feeding sharks and rays to minimize any potential negative impacts on their natural behavior and feeding patterns.

b) Education and Awareness: Many excursion operators take the opportunity to educate visitors about the importance of marine conservation, the challenges faced by these creatures, and what individuals can do to help protect them.

c) Research and Data Collection: Some organizations collaborate with marine biologists to conduct research and gather data on shark and ray populations. This information helps inform conservation efforts and aids in the understanding of these marine species' behavior and migration patterns.

d) Limits on Tour Numbers: To prevent overcrowding and undue stress on marine life, the number of participants on each excursion is often limited.

Essential Tips for a Safe and Memorable Visit:

Participating in a shark and ray feeding excursion in Bora Bora is an extraordinary adventure, but it's crucial to prioritize safety and the well-being of marine life. Here are some essential tips for visitors:

a) Choose a Reputable Operator: Research and select a tour operator with a strong commitment to eco-tourism practices and responsible wildlife interactions.

b) Listen to the Guides: Pay close attention to the safety briefing provided by the guides and follow their instructions at all times.

c) Respect the Marine Life: Maintain a safe distance from the sharks and rays and avoid touching or disturbing them. Remember, they are wild animals, and our presence should not disrupt their natural behavior.

d) Use Eco-Friendly Sunscreen: When swimming in the lagoon, use reef-safe sunscreen to avoid harmful chemicals from entering the water and potentially harming marine life.

e) Capture Memories Respectfully: If you bring a camera or underwater device, be mindful not to stress the animals while taking photos or videos.

Jet Ski Tours

The Allure of Jet Ski Tours in Bora Bora

Bora Bora's picturesque lagoon, encircled by the protective barrier reef, offers the perfect playground for jet ski enthusiasts. Jet ski tours allow visitors to explore the island's breathtaking natural landscapes and experience the thrill of gliding across crystal-clear waters, making for an unforgettable adventure. Whether it's the scenic view of Mount Otemanu, the vibrant coral gardens, or the mesmerizing marine life, the beauty of Bora Bora is magnified tenfold when explored on a jet ski.

Tour Options: From Short Excursions to Full-Day Adventures

Jet ski tours in Bora Bora come in various forms, catering to different preferences and interests. For those short on time or new to jet skiing, introductory tours offer a taste of the experience, typically lasting one to two hours. These tours often focus on exploring the lagoon's highlights, such as the famous coral gardens and small islets.

For more experienced riders looking for an in-depth adventure, full-day tours are an excellent choice. These tours may encompass the entire circumference of the island, allowing participants to discover hidden coves, snorkeling spots, and even visit other nearby islands. Depending on the tour operator, lunch might be provided on a secluded beach, enhancing the overall experience.

Safety First: Guidelines and Precautions

While jet ski tours are exhilarating, safety remains a top priority. Before embarking on any tour, participants receive comprehensive safety briefings from professional guides. These briefings cover the proper use of jet skis, safety protocols, navigation rules, and information on sensitive areas to avoid, such as coral reefs and marine sanctuaries.

Life jackets are mandatory, and riders are encouraged to wear protective gear like wetsuits and rash guards, especially during longer tours. Speed limits are often imposed in certain areas to safeguard marine life and prevent damage to the fragile ecosystem.

Best Time to Visit Bora Bora for Jet Ski Tours

Bora Bora boasts a tropical climate, with warm temperatures year-round. However, certain times of the year may be more favorable for jet ski tours based on weather conditions and marine life activity.

The dry season, spanning from May to October, offers the most consistent weather and calm waters, making it an ideal time for jet skiing. With lower chances of rainfall and storms, visitors can enjoy clearer skies and better visibility underwater. The months of July and August, though slightly cooler, are particularly popular among tourists seeking a seamless jet ski experience.

Environmental Impact and Conservation Efforts

As with any tourism-related activity, jet ski tours can have an impact on the environment. One of the most significant concerns is the potential damage to coral reefs and marine life due to accidental collisions or reckless behavior. To address these issues, local authorities and tour operators have implemented strict guidelines and regulations.

Many tour companies are actively involved in conservation efforts, promoting responsible tourism and encouraging visitors to respect the delicate marine ecosystem. Initiatives such as beach clean-ups and educational programs aim to raise awareness about the importance of preserving Bora Bora's natural beauty for future generations.

Supporting Local Economy through Responsible Tourism

Jet ski tours also play a vital role in supporting the local economy of Bora Bora. The tourism industry is a major contributor to the island's economy, providing employment opportunities and sustaining businesses. By participating in jet ski tours, visitors contribute directly to the livelihoods of local guides, operators, and other related businesses.

Furthermore, responsible tourism practices, such as supporting locally owned and operated tour companies, can have a positive impact on the overall well-being of the community. By fostering a sustainable tourism industry, Bora Bora can continue to thrive while preserving its unique cultural heritage and natural wonders.

Sailing and Boat Trips

1. Bora Bora's Nautical Paradise

Bora Bora's nautical paradise is a dream come true for sailing enthusiasts and water lovers alike. The island is surrounded by a vibrant coral reef, creating a tranquil lagoon that's perfect for sailing and boat excursions. Visitors can embark on journeys of discovery, exploring the island's hidden gems, lush landscapes, and fascinating marine life.

2. Sailing Options in Bora Bora

a. Chartering a Yacht

For those seeking an opulent and personalized sailing experience, chartering a private yacht is the ultimate way to explore Bora Bora's beauty. Numerous charter companies operate on the island, offering a wide range of yachts catering to various group sizes and budgets. A yacht charter allows visitors to tailor their itinerary, choosing from an array of destinations such as Matira Point, Coral Gardens, and the famous Mount Otemanu.

b. Catamaran Sailing

Catamaran sailing is another popular option, especially for groups or families. Catamarans are stable, spacious vessels that provide a comfortable and safe sailing experience. Many local operators offer catamaran rentals, complete with experienced crew members to ensure a memorable and hassle-free journey.

c. Traditional Polynesian Canoe Sailing

For travelers seeking an authentic experience, traditional Polynesian canoe sailing is a must-try. Hop on a Vaka Moana, a traditional outrigger canoe, and be enchanted by the rhythmic paddling while gazing at the horizon. These sailing trips often come with cultural insights and storytelling by local guides, providing a deeper connection to the island's heritage.

3. Boat Trips and Excursions

a. Sunset Cruises

Bora Bora's sunsets are unparalleled, and a sunset cruise is the perfect way to bask in their splendor. Many boat operators offer guided sunset cruises, where visitors can relax with a tropical cocktail in hand and watch as the sky transforms into a palette of vibrant hues.

b. Snorkeling and Diving Excursions

The underwater world around Bora Bora is teeming with marine life, making snorkeling and diving a must-do activity. Many boat trips include stops at prime snorkeling and diving spots, such as the Coral Gardens and Anau, where visitors can swim alongside colorful fish, rays, and sometimes even sharks.

c. Shark and Ray Feeding Tours

Bora Bora is known for its friendly black-tip reef sharks and stingrays. Shark and ray feeding tours are thrilling experiences, allowing visitors to get up close and personal with these fascinating creatures while learning about their conservation.

d. Motu Picnics

Motus are small islets surrounding Bora Bora's lagoon, and many boat trips offer idyllic motu picnics. Visitors can savor local delicacies, relax on pristine beaches, and take in the breathtaking views of the mainland.

e. Lagoon Tours

Lagoon tours are comprehensive excursions that provide a well-rounded experience of Bora Bora's beauty. These tours often include stops at various points of interest, like the Faanui Canon, Matira Beach, and World War II remnants.

4. Practical Tips and Considerations

a. Best Time to Visit

Bora Bora's tropical climate means that visitors can enjoy sailing and boat trips throughout the year. However, the dry season, which spans from May to October, is generally considered the best time to visit due to milder weather and lower rainfall.

b. Safety Measures

While sailing and boat trips are generally safe, it's essential to adhere to safety guidelines and listen to the instructions of experienced crew members. Always wear appropriate safety gear, including life jackets, especially during water-based activities.

c. Booking in Advance

Due to Bora Bora's popularity, it is advisable to book sailing trips and boat excursions in advance, particularly during peak tourist seasons. This ensures availability and prevents disappointment.

d. Respect for the Environment

Bora Bora's delicate ecosystem and coral reefs require responsible tourism. Visitors should refrain

conditions can change rapidly, and hikers should be well-prepared with proper gear, sufficient water, and sturdy hiking boots. The hike usually takes around 6 to 8 hours, depending on the chosen route and the hiker's pace.

Upon reaching the summit, hikers are rewarded with a breathtaking 360-degree view of Bora Bora's emerald lagoon, the surrounding motus (small islets), and the vast expanse of the Pacific Ocean. The experience of witnessing the sunrise or sunset from this vantage point is nothing short of awe-inspiring and is sure to create lasting memories.

2. Matira Point Trail: A Relaxing Stroll Along the Coastline

For visitors seeking a more leisurely nature walk, the Matira Point Trail offers a serene experience along the island's southern coast. This easy-going trail stretches for approximately 2 kilometers (1.2 miles) and takes hikers through coconut palm groves and pristine white-sand beaches.

The trail starts near the famous Matira Beach, known for its stunning sunsets and shallow, crystal-clear waters. Hikers can explore the beach and then continue along the coast, enjoying views of the turquoise lagoon on one side and lush vegetation on the other. The Matira Point Trail is an ideal spot for photography enthusiasts, as it offers numerous picturesque vistas.

As the trail meanders along the coastline, hikers may encounter locals fishing or enjoying picnics with their families. This presents an excellent opportunity for cultural exchange and learning about the traditional ways of life on the island.

3. Faanui Valley Trail: Discovering Bora Bora's Tropical Flora and Fauna

The Faanui Valley Trail is a nature lover's delight, offering a chance to immerse oneself in the island's rich biodiversity. This moderate-level hike takes visitors through the verdant Faanui Valley, which is nestled between the majestic peaks of Mount Pahia and Mount Otemanu.

The trail begins at the village of Faanui and leads hikers through dense tropical vegetation, including lush ferns, bamboo groves, and exotic flowers. The trail is dotted with several small waterfalls and streams, adding to the scenic beauty of the journey.

Along the way, visitors may spot native bird species, such as the Tahitian reed-warbler and the blue lorikeet. For birdwatchers and wildlife enthusiasts, it's a perfect opportunity to observe these creatures in their natural habitat.

As the trail gains elevation, it offers sweeping views of the surrounding landscapes and the lagoon. The ascent is moderately steep in some sections, but it is achievable for most hikers with average fitness levels. It's recommended to bring insect repellent and wear light, breathable clothing during the hike.

4. Mount Pahia Hike: A Thrilling Climb to Another Summit

Similar to Mount Otemanu, Mount Pahia is a volcanic peak on Bora Bora, offering another challenging hiking opportunity for experienced climbers. Though it is slightly shorter than Mount Otemanu, standing at 661 meters (2,169 feet) above sea level, it presents a more technical ascent, making it suitable for seasoned hikers and climbers.

The trail to Mount Pahia begins near the village of Fitiiu and involves steep ascents, rock scrambling, and the use of ropes in certain sections. Because of the technical nature of this hike, it is highly recommended to undertake it with a certified guide and to have prior experience in mountain climbing or rappelling.

The reward for those who conquer Mount Pahia is the breathtaking view from the summit, which includes an unrivaled perspective of Mount Otemanu and the lush valleys below. The rugged terrain and adrenaline-inducing climb make this hike a memorable adventure for outdoor enthusiasts seeking a thrilling experience.

5. Motu Tapu: An Island Paradise Within an Island Paradise

While not a traditional hiking trail, a visit to Motu Tapu offers a unique opportunity to explore a pristine private islet just a short boat ride away from the main island of Bora Bora. Motu Tapu is often referred to as the "Private Island," as it was once exclusively reserved for Polynesian royalty.

Visitors can arrange a boat excursion to this secluded paradise and spend a day in absolute tranquility surrounded by powdery white sands and crystal-clear waters. The turquoise lagoon surrounding Motu Tapu is ideal for snorkeling, swimming, and simply basking in the sun.

A leisurely stroll around the islet reveals an abundance of natural beauty, including native plants, seabirds, and marine life. It's also an excellent spot for a romantic picnic or a private moment of solitude amidst the captivating landscape.

6. Tips for Hiking and Nature Walks in Bora Bora

While exploring the hiking trails and nature walks in Bora Bora, visitors should keep the following tips in mind:

a. Respect the Environment: Bora Bora's natural beauty is fragile and should be treated with care. Avoid leaving any litter behind and refrain from touching or disturbing the flora and fauna.

b. Stay Hydrated: The tropical climate of Bora Bora can be hot and humid, especially during the peak season. Carry sufficient water and stay hydrated throughout your hikes.

c. Wear Appropriate Footwear: Sturdy and comfortable hiking shoes are essential for tackling the rugged terrain of some trails. Sandals or flip-flops may not provide adequate support and may cause discomfort.

d. Sun Protection: The island experiences strong sunlight, so wear sunscreen, a wide-brimmed hat, and sunglasses to protect yourself from harmful UV rays.

e. Insect Repellent: Biting insects are common in tropical environments, so apply insect repellent to avoid uncomfortable encounters.

f. Know Your Limits: Some hikes, like those to Mount Otemanu and Mount Pahia, can be physically demanding. Be honest about your fitness level and choose trails that match your abilities.

g. Hire a Local Guide: For a more enriching experience and added safety, consider hiring a licensed local guide who can provide valuable insights into the island's culture, history, and natural heritage.

4x4 Safari Expeditions

Bora Bora's Breathtaking Landscape:

Bora Bora boasts a lush and diverse landscape that beckons exploration. The 4x4 safari expeditions allow visitors to traverse rugged terrain and experience the island's untamed beauty firsthand. From volcanic peaks and dense jungles to scenic overlooks and pristine valleys, the island's landscape is a photographer's dream.

Mount Otemanu: The Crown Jewel:

At the heart of Bora Bora lies Mount Otemanu, an extinct volcano that towers over the island at 2,385 feet (727 meters). The 4x4 safari expeditions take visitors on a thrilling ride up the mountain, providing panoramic views of the surrounding lagoon and neighboring islets. Along the way, expert guides share fascinating stories about the island's geology and cultural significance.

Faanui Valley:

The Faanui Valley is a hidden gem within Bora Bora, showcasing the island's rich flora and fauna. 4x4 safaris venture into this lush wilderness, where visitors can encounter native plant species, vibrant tropical flowers, and exotic birdlife. The valley's serenity offers a stark contrast to the bustling beachfronts, providing a serene escape for nature enthusiasts.

II. Immerse in Local Culture:

Interaction with Friendly Locals:

Bora Bora's warm and welcoming locals add a unique dimension to the 4x4 safari experience. Along the way, visitors have the opportunity to interact with residents and gain insights into their traditional way of life, folklore, and cultural practices. This cultural exchange enhances the safari journey and creates lasting memories for the travelers.

Visiting Ancient Marae:

During the 4x4 safari expeditions, visitors can explore ancient marae, sacred Polynesian temples once used for religious and social gatherings. The guides share stories about these historical sites, connecting the past and present while fostering a deeper appreciation for the island's cultural heritage.

III. Thrilling Adventure and Outdoor Activities:

Off-Road Thrills:

The 4x4 safari expeditions take visitors off the beaten path and into the heart of the island's wilderness. Driving on rugged trails and crossing rocky terrains offer an adrenaline rush for adventure seekers. With experienced drivers at the helm, the safaris ensure a safe yet thrilling experience for all participants.

Breathtaking Viewpoints:

Bora Bora's interior is adorned with several breathtaking viewpoints that provide awe-inspiring vistas of the island's lagoon and motus (islets). These viewpoints are often inaccessible by foot, making the 4x4 safaris the ideal way to reach them and capture picture-perfect moments.

IV. Ecological Awareness and Sustainability:

Responsible Tourism:

As Bora Bora strives to maintain its pristine environment, 4x4 safari expeditions embrace principles of responsible tourism. Eco-friendly vehicles are used to minimize the impact on the delicate ecosystem, ensuring that future generations can also enjoy the island's natural beauty.

Education and Awareness:

The 4x4 safari guides play a crucial role in educating visitors about the island's fragile ecosystem and the importance of conservation efforts. This hands-on experience fosters a deeper connection with nature and raises awareness about the need to protect Bora Bora's unique biodiversity.

Polynesian Cultural Tours

The Significance of Polynesian Culture in Bora Bora:

Polynesian culture plays a fundamental role in shaping the identity of Bora Bora, reflecting the island's heritage and ancestral roots. The Polynesians are renowned for their artistry, dance, music, oral traditions, and sacred rituals, which have been passed down through generations. These cultural tours offer a unique opportunity to witness and participate in age-old practices, fostering a deep appreciation for the local way of life.

Cultural Tour Itinerary Highlights:

A. Traditional Welcome Ceremony: Upon arriving in Bora Bora, tourists are greeted with a traditional welcome ceremony, where locals perform a mesmerizing dance and offer fragrant flower leis as a symbol of warmth and hospitality. This sets the tone for an unforgettable cultural journey.

B. Tāmūrē Dance Lessons: Tāmūrē, a dynamic and rhythmic dance form, holds significant importance in Polynesian culture. Tourists get the chance to partake in dance lessons conducted by expert dancers, learning the graceful movements and lively beats of this ancient art.

C. Exploring Marae Sites: Marae sites are sacred places where important ceremonies and rituals were once held by Polynesian ancestors. The tour takes visitors to these historical spots, providing insights into the island's spiritual beliefs and cultural practices.

D. Art and Craft Workshops: Engaging in art and craft workshops, tourists can try their hand at traditional activities like weaving coconut leaves, creating flower crowns, and carving intricate designs on wood, a skill passed down through generations.

E. Traditional Cuisine Experience: Food plays a vital role in any culture, and Polynesian cuisine is no exception. Tourists are treated to authentic meals prepared with fresh, locally-sourced ingredients, providing a delectable insight into the island's culinary delights.

F. Outrigger Canoe Excursions: Exploring Bora Bora's crystalline lagoon on an outrigger canoe is a highlight of the cultural tour. This traditional form of transportation was once the lifeline of Polynesian communities, and tourists can relish the panoramic views and bond with their local guides.

Cultural Preservation and Sustainability:

Polynesian cultural tours in Bora Bora also play a crucial role in cultural preservation and sustainability. By actively participating in these tours, visitors contribute to the preservation of traditional practices and provide economic support to local communities, encouraging them to maintain their way of life and protect their natural surroundings.

Impact on Tourists:

Participating in Polynesian cultural tours leaves a lasting impact on tourists, transcending the realm of a mere vacation. Tourists often develop a deep sense of respect for the Polynesian culture and its connection to nature, recognizing the value of preserving indigenous knowledge and heritage worldwide.

Helicopter Tours - A Bird's Eye View

Benefits of Helicopter Tours in Bora Bora

Helicopter tours offer a range of benefits that set them apart from other modes of sightseeing on the island. Let's explore some of these advantages:

Aerial Vantage Point: Viewing Bora Bora's natural wonders from the air provides an unparalleled vantage point. Passengers can witness the breathtaking colors of the lagoon, the picturesque islets, and the majestic Mount Otemanu all in one panoramic view.

Accessibility to Remote Areas: Many parts of Bora Bora's beauty are inaccessible by land or boat. Helicopter tours open up opportunities to explore hidden waterfalls, pristine beaches, and secluded spots that are otherwise difficult to reach.

Time Efficiency: With limited time on a vacation, helicopter tours offer the chance to cover a significant portion of the island in a short period. Travelers can maximize their sightseeing experience without sacrificing precious hours.

Safety and Comfort: Reputable helicopter tour operators prioritize passenger safety and provide comfortable seating for an enjoyable flight experience.

Photographic Opportunities: Photographers and enthusiasts will relish the chance to capture unique aerial shots of Bora Bora's natural beauty, making for unforgettable memories.

Popular Helicopter Tour Routes

Several captivating routes are available to visitors, each offering a distinct experience. Here are some of the most popular helicopter tour routes in Bora Bora:

Circle Island Tour: This classic tour takes visitors on a thrilling ride around the entire island. Passengers can marvel at the diverse landscapes, coral reefs, and the awe-inspiring Mount Otemanu from all angles.

Mount Otemanu and Valley of the Kings: For those seeking a more adventurous journey, this tour takes you up close to Mount Otemanu, the dormant volcano that dominates the island's skyline. Additionally, visitors can explore the mystical Valley of the Kings, an ancient site of cultural significance.

Overwater Bungalows Tour: A must for those staying in the luxurious overwater bungalows, this tour allows guests to witness the unique charm of their accommodations from the air.

Sunset Helicopter Tour: Ideal for couples and romantics, this tour takes flight during the golden hour, offering a spectacular view of the sun setting over the Pacific Ocean.

Incredible Sights to Behold

As the helicopter soars above Bora Bora, visitors are treated to a mesmerizing array of sights. Some of the must-see attractions include:

Bora Bora Lagoon: The island's crystal-clear lagoon, teeming with colorful marine life, is a sight to behold from above. The mesmerizing shades of blue and green create an unforgettable visual experience.

Coral Reefs: Bora Bora is renowned for its vibrant coral reefs. From the helicopter, passengers can observe the intricate patterns and vibrant colors of the reefs beneath the water's surface.

Matira Beach: Considered one of the world's most beautiful beaches, Matira Beach's white sands and turquoise waters create a stunning contrast that captivates from above.

Mount Otemanu: As the island's highest peak, Mount Otemanu's majestic presence dominates the landscape, offering an awe-inspiring view for passengers.

Motu Islands: Bora Bora is surrounded by small, sandy islets known as motus. From the helicopter, visitors can witness the allure of these islets and their exclusive overwater resorts.

Tips for an Unforgettable Helicopter Tour Experience

To make the most of their helicopter tour in Bora Bora, visitors should keep in mind the following tips:

Book in Advance: Helicopter tours are popular, so it's advisable to book well in advance to secure a spot and potentially get better deals.

Choose Reputable Operators: Ensure you select a reputable helicopter tour operator with experienced pilots and a strong safety record.

Dress Comfortably: Wear comfortable clothing and shoes that allow ease of movement during the tour.

GoPro or Camera: Don't forget to bring a camera or GoPro to capture the awe-inspiring aerial views.

Listen to the Guide: Pay attention to the pilot's instructions and commentary throughout the tour to fully appreciate the sights.

CHAPTER SIX:INDULGE IN BORA BORA'S CUISINE

Local Delicacies and Must-Try Dishes

Apart from its natural beauty, Bora Bora offers a delightful culinary experience that reflects the vibrant culture of the region. From fresh seafood to tropical fruits, the island's local delicacies showcase a fusion of French, Polynesian, and international influences. Let me take you on a gastronomic journey through the must-try dishes and local delicacies in Bora Bora, enticing visitors to indulge in the flavors of this tropical paradise.

1. Poisson Cru: Poisson Cru, or raw fish, is a quintessential dish in French Polynesia. It is often considered the national dish of the region and is prepared using freshly caught tuna or other local fish. The fish is marinated in lime juice and mixed with coconut milk, diced vegetables like tomatoes, cucumbers, and onions, and sometimes grated carrots. The tangy and refreshing flavors of Poisson Cru make it a perfect choice for warm tropical days.

2. I'a Ota: Similar to Poisson Cru, I'a Ota is another raw fish preparation. It features various types of fish, such as mahi-mahi, marlin, or parrotfish, mixed with coconut milk, lime juice, and fragrant Tahitian herbs. The addition of freshly grated coconut gives it a unique texture and enhances the tropical taste.

3. E'ia Ota: For seafood enthusiasts, E'ia Ota is a treat not to be missed. This dish consists of small pieces of raw fish mixed with freshly squeezed lime juice, diced vegetables, and a selection of aromatic spices. The mixture is often served in a coconut shell, adding to the island vibe and presentation.

4. Pua'a Roti: As Bora Bora embraces French influences, Pua'a Roti showcases a delicious blend of local and French flavors. This dish features succulent, slow-cooked pork wrapped in a soft, flaky pastry similar to a croissant. The result is a mouthwatering treat that highlights the island's fusion of culinary influences.

5. Po'e: For those with a sweet tooth, Po'e is a traditional Polynesian dessert that won't disappoint. This pudding-like delight is made from mashed ripe bananas, grated pumpkin or sweet potato, coconut milk, and vanilla, all wrapped in banana leaves and baked to perfection. The result is a scrumptious and comforting dessert that reflects the island's tropical flavors.

6. Mahi-Mahi: When it comes to seafood, Mahi-Mahi is a popular choice among locals and visitors alike. Also known as dolphinfish, this fish is a delicacy in Bora Bora due to its firm, succulent texture and mild flavor. It is often grilled or pan-seared and served with a side of fresh vegetables or tropical fruit salsa, making it a delectable option for seafood lovers.

7. Grilled Lobster: Bora Bora's pristine waters are home to an abundance of lobsters, and grilled lobster is a must-try dish for any visitor. The succulent lobster is lightly seasoned, grilled to perfection, and served with a side of garlic butter or a tangy dipping sauce, allowing the natural flavors of the lobster to shine.

8. Firi Firi: Firi Firi is a delightful Polynesian treat that resembles donut holes. Made from a simple dough of flour, water, and yeast, these golden-brown delights are fried until they achieve a fluffy, airy texture. Firi Firi is often enjoyed as a breakfast item or as a sweet snack throughout the day.

9. Tahitian Vanilla Products: Bora Bora is renowned for producing some of the world's finest vanilla, and visitors should take advantage of this opportunity to indulge in vanilla-infused delights. Look for vanilla-based products such as vanilla-infused coffee, ice cream, rum, and even body products like lotions and scrubs.

10. Local Tropical Fruits: Bora Bora is a treasure trove of tropical fruits, and sampling the island's diverse offerings is a must for any foodie. Try the luscious pineapple, papaya, mango, coconut, passion fruit, and breadfruit, among others. You'll be enchanted by the natural sweetness and unique flavors of these locally grown fruits.

11. Tamure: Tamure is not a dish but a traditional Tahitian dance often performed during special occasions and events. However, it's worth mentioning because it reflects the vibrant Polynesian culture and is often accompanied by feasting and traditional food offerings, providing visitors with a complete cultural experience.

12. Tama'ara'a: This unique delicacy showcases the island's abundance of seafood. Tama'ara'a is a traditional Tahitian seafood salad featuring various cooked fish, octopus, and other shellfish. The seafood is mixed with vegetables, fresh coconut, and a dressing made from lime juice and grated coconut, resulting in a delightful and colorful dish.

13. Roasted Pig (Lechon): During special occasions and traditional feasts, locals prepare a roasted pig known as "lechon." The whole pig is slow-roasted over an open fire, creating tender, flavorful meat with crispy skin. This communal feast is a wonderful way for visitors to immerse themselves in Polynesian hospitality and traditions.

14. Pineapple and Coconut Sorbet: Given the abundance of tropical fruits on the island, you'll find some delectable fruit-based desserts, such as pineapple and coconut sorbet. These refreshing treats are perfect for cooling off in the tropical heat while enjoying the flavors of the region.

15. Bora Bora Cocktail: To complete your culinary journey, indulge in the signature Bora Bora cocktail. Made from a mix of local fruit juices, rum, and sometimes coconut cream, this delightful concoction encapsulates the essence of the island's tropical paradise.

Popular Restaurants and Dining Spots

1. St. James Restaurant

Situated on the southern tip of Bora Bora, St. James Restaurant is a celebrated culinary gem that captures the essence of French and Polynesian fusion cuisine. The restaurant's panoramic views of Mount Otemanu and the turquoise lagoon create a magical setting for a memorable dining experience. Their talented chefs skillfully blend locally sourced ingredients with

French culinary techniques, resulting in an array of delectable dishes.

The menu boasts a wide selection of seafood delicacies, including freshly caught fish and succulent shellfish. One of their signature dishes is "Tuna Tartare with Coconut Milk and Lime," which perfectly showcases the island's abundant marine resources and culinary creativity. For those who prefer a meaty option, the "Vanilla and Ginger-Glazed Pork Tenderloin" is a must-try, tender and full of unique flavors.

2. Bora Bora Yacht Club

For travelers seeking a more laid-back, beachfront dining experience, the Bora Bora Yacht Club is a prime choice. Located on the Matira Point Beach, this charming establishment offers stunning views of the lagoon and the setting sun. With its casual ambiance and warm hospitality, the Yacht Club is a popular spot among locals and visitors alike.

The menu features an assortment of Mediterranean-inspired dishes, emphasizing fresh produce and seafood. Their wood-fired pizzas, with a touch of local ingredients, are renowned for their crispy crust and delectable toppings. Pair your meal with a refreshing cocktail or a glass of wine from their extensive selection, and you have the perfect recipe for a delightful evening by the water's edge.

3. Bloody Mary's

No visit to Bora Bora is complete without stopping by Bloody Mary's, an iconic and legendary restaurant that has welcomed celebrities, dignitaries, and curious travelers for decades. Known for its unique, sand-floored dining area and rustic, laid-back atmosphere, this restaurant has become a must-visit destination on the island.

Bloody Mary's offers an intriguing mix of international and Polynesian dishes, with a focus on fresh, locally sourced ingredients. The "Freshly Grilled Fish of the Day" and the "Marinated Tahitian Fish Salad" are perennial favorites among seafood enthusiasts. Moreover, the restaurant's open-air bar boasts an impressive selection of tropical cocktails, including their signature "Bloody Mary" cocktail, served with a generous garnish of local flavors.

4. La Villa Mahana

For an intimate and exclusive dining experience, La Villa Mahana stands out as a culinary gem. This small, family-run restaurant accommodates only a handful of guests per night, ensuring personalized attention and a unique culinary journey.

Chef Damien Rinaldi Dovio, who gained fame through his appearances on international cooking shows, curates an ever-changing menu that showcases the freshest and finest ingredients available. Each dish is a work of art, carefully crafted to stimulate the senses. The "Foie Gras with Tropical Fruits" and the "Vanilla Lobster with Sweet Potato Puree" exemplify the chef's expertise in combining French techniques with local ingredients.

5. Matira Beach Restaurant

For those seeking a delightful beachfront dining experience with toes in the sand, Matira Beach Restaurant is the ideal spot. Situated on the popular Matira Beach, this restaurant offers stunning views of the lagoon and the mesmerizing sunset.

The restaurant's menu revolves around classic Polynesian dishes and international favorites, catering to a wide range of tastes. The "Poisson Cru" (raw fish marinated in coconut milk and lime) is a must-try traditional dish that captures the essence of Polynesian cuisine. The "Grilled Lobster" is another crowd-pleaser, showcasing the island's abundant seafood.

6. Lagoon Restaurant by Jean-Georges

For epicureans seeking a high-end, fine dining experience, the Lagoon Restaurant by Jean-Georges is a premier choice. Part of the luxurious St. Regis Bora Bora Resort, this culinary gem is helmed by world-renowned chef Jean-Georges Vongerichten.

The restaurant's setting is nothing short of spectacular, with a deck extending over the lagoon, offering panoramic views of Mount Otemanu and the surrounding waters. The menu boasts a fusion of French and Asian flavors, creating an exciting and innovative dining experience. Dishes like the "Spicy Tuna Tartare" and the "Black Pepper and Soy-Glazed Mahi-Mahi" exemplify the chef's talent in blending global influences with local ingredients.

7. Fare Manuia

Fare Manuia, located on the main island of Bora Bora, offers a genuine taste of traditional Polynesian fare in a serene and picturesque setting. The open-air, thatched-roof restaurant overlooks a tranquil garden, creating a laid-back and authentic ambiance.

The menu features an array of Polynesian classics, with dishes like "Pua'a Roti" (roasted pork) and "Po'e" (a traditional banana and coconut dessert). Visitors have the opportunity to savor the flavors of ancient recipes passed down through generations. The restaurant also hosts traditional Polynesian dance performances and live music, enhancing the cultural experience.

8. La Matira Beach Restaurant & Bar

Situated on the eastern side of Matira Point, La Matira Beach Restaurant & Bar offers an idyllic beachfront dining experience with breathtaking views of the lagoon and its turquoise waters.

The menu highlights the island's fresh seafood, grilled to perfection and served with flavorful accompaniments. The "Grilled Octopus with Mango Chutney" and the "Tuna Steak with Lemon Butter Sauce" are highly recommended dishes for seafood enthusiasts. The restaurant's friendly and welcoming staff ensure a delightful dining experience, making it a popular spot among both locals and tourists.

9. Manu Tuki

Located on the Motu Toopua islet, Manu Tuki offers a fine dining experience in a mesmerizing setting overlooking the lagoon and Mount Otemanu. This exclusive restaurant prides itself on offering organic, locally sourced ingredients and authentic Polynesian flavors.

The menu changes frequently, depending on the availability of fresh produce and seafood. Dishes like "Tahitian Vanilla and Lemongrass Scallops" and "Pineapple Glazed Duck Breast" exemplify the chef's creativity in combining traditional Polynesian ingredients with modern culinary techniques.

10. Kaina Hut

For travelers seeking a casual and affordable dining experience, Kaina Hut is a favorite among locals and visitors alike. Situated near the Bora Bora Yacht Club, this charming eatery offers a menu that combines French and Polynesian influences.

The "Grilled Mahi-Mahi Burger" and the "Seafood Platter" are among the restaurant's popular dishes. With a laid-back ambiance and friendly staff, Kaina Hut provides a delightful spot to unwind and enjoy the island's culinary delights.

Experiencing a Traditional Polynesian Feast

The Significance of Polynesian Feasts:

Polynesian feasts, also known as 'luaus' in some regions, hold great cultural importance for the people of Bora Bora. They are deeply rooted in their history and traditions, serving as a means of gathering and fostering communal bonds. These feasts mark significant events, such as weddings, births, harvest celebrations, and other important milestones, showcasing the vibrant and diverse Polynesian culture.

Preparations for the Feast:

Organizing a traditional Polynesian feast is a laborious and collective effort that involves the entire community. Weeks before the event, villagers come together to prepare for the grand occasion. From crafting decorative elements like colorful flower garlands (lei) and hand-woven mats to procuring fresh ingredients for the feast, every aspect is carefully considered. The main dish, known as "umu," is a delicious blend of vegetables, fruits, seafood, and meat, cooked in an earth oven to perfection.

Welcoming the Guests:

On the day of the feast, visitors are greeted with warm smiles, traditional songs, and the rhythmic beat of drums as they step foot on the sandy shores of Bora Bora. The locals are dressed in their finest traditional attire, adorned with flowers, shells, and vibrant fabrics, reflecting the island's radiant spirit.

Embracing the Polynesian Culture:

As the evening progresses, guests are invited to participate in various cultural activities. Learning the art of Hula dance, trying their hand at coconut husking, and playing traditional Polynesian games enable visitors to connect with the island's heritage on a deeper level. Local artisans showcase their craftsmanship, offering handmade crafts and jewelry that serve as memorable souvenirs of this enchanting experience.

The Feast Unveiled:

As the sun sets, a mesmerizing aroma fills the air as the grand feast is unveiled. The 'umu' is opened, revealing an abundance of delectable dishes, each prepared with care and expertise. Freshly caught fish, succulent pork, flavorful taro, and an array of tropical fruits tantalize the taste buds of the guests, creating a symphony of flavors.

Cultural Performances:

While enjoying the feast, guests are treated to a dazzling display of Polynesian dances and performances. The energetic drum beats, graceful movements of the dancers, and the colorful costumes transport the audience to a world of ancient legends and tales. The mesmerizing fire dance, in particular, captivates everyone as skilled performers twirl fire poi, leaving trails of light in the night sky.

Cultural Significance of Food:

In Polynesian culture, food holds a sacred significance. Each dish represents a connection to the land, sea, and ancestors. As guests savor the delicacies, they partake in a spiritual journey that honors the island's bountiful nature and the generations that have passed down these culinary traditions.

Sharing Stories and Legends:

After the performances, elders of the community often gather guests around a bonfire to share ancient stories and legends that have been passed down through generations. These stories shed light on the cultural values, beliefs, and the deep bond between the people and their surroundings.

Spirit of Togetherness:

The most profound aspect of a traditional Polynesian feast is the sense of togetherness it fosters. As guests from different corners of the world come together to celebrate, they become part of a larger family, united by their shared experience and appreciation for Polynesian culture.

CHAPTER SEVEN:SHOPPING IN BORA BORA

Souvenirs and Handicrafts

Introduction to Bora Bora Souvenirs and Handicrafts:

When visiting Bora Bora, one cannot help but be captivated by the island's rich cultural heritage. The local artisans take immense pride in their craft, showcasing their talents through various souvenirs and handicrafts. These unique creations are not only beautiful but also hold sentimental value, serving as cherished reminders of the island's beauty and warmth.

1. The Art of Tahitian Pearls:

Tahitian pearls are some of the most sought-after treasures in Bora Bora. These lustrous gems, cultivated from the black-lipped oyster, are admired for their stunning array of colors, ranging from dark green and peacock blue to silver and black. Visitors can purchase Tahitian pearl jewelry, including necklaces, earrings, and bracelets, in the island's boutiques and markets. These exquisite pieces not only make for exceptional souvenirs but also symbolize purity and elegance.

2. Handwoven Crafts:

Bora Bora's artisans are highly skilled in the art of weaving, using pandanus leaves and coconut fronds to create beautiful and practical items. One popular handicraft is the "tifaifai," a traditional quilt made by stitching together intricate patterns on vibrant fabrics. Tifaifai is a symbol of Polynesian culture and is often passed down through generations. Tourists can find tifaifai in various sizes, making them ideal for home decor or as unique wall hangings.

3. Wood Carvings:

Wood carving is another prominent form of artistic expression in Bora Bora. Local carvers use tropical woods like mahogany, rosewood, and tamanu to create stunning sculptures and decorative items. From intricately detailed statues depicting Polynesian gods and goddesses to practical items like bowls and utensils, these wooden crafts embody the island's cultural significance and connection to nature.

4. Polynesian Tattoos:

Tattooing holds deep cultural significance in Polynesia, and Bora Bora is no exception. For those seeking a more personalized souvenir, traditional Polynesian tattoos, known as "tatau," can be a unique and meaningful choice. These tattoos often feature intricate patterns and symbols that tell stories of the wearer's heritage and personal journey.

5. Pareos and Sarongs:

The colorful and stylish pareos and sarongs are a must-have when visiting Bora Bora. These versatile garments can be worn as wraps, skirts, dresses, or used as beach towels. Local artisans handprint these fabrics using traditional methods, showcasing a wide array of tropical motifs, such as hibiscus flowers, marine life, and tribal designs.

6. Seashell Creations:

Given Bora Bora's pristine beaches, it is no surprise that seashell creations are abundant in the island's souvenir shops. Local artists utilize various shells, coral, and pearls to craft stunning jewelry, decorative items, and ornaments. Seashell necklaces, bracelets, and earrings make for exquisite and lightweight keepsakes that embody the island's coastal charm.

7. Vanilla Products:

Bora Bora is well-known for its premium vanilla production. Visitors can indulge in the island's delicious vanilla-infused treats like cookies, jams, and liqueurs. Moreover, they can purchase vanilla beans and extract, offering a unique taste of Bora Bora to savor even after returning home.

8. Local Paintings and Artwork:

The island's breathtaking landscapes and vibrant culture have inspired many local artists to create stunning paintings and artwork. Scenes of crystal-clear lagoons, lush mountains, and Tahitian dances often take center stage in these artistic representations. Purchasing a painting or artwork not only supports local talent but also allows visitors to take a piece of Bora Bora's natural beauty with them.

9. Coconut-Based Products:

Coconut trees are abundant in Bora Bora, and the locals ingeniously use different parts of the tree to create various products. From coconut oil for skincare to coconut-based snacks and beverages, visitors can explore a wide range of coconut-based souvenirs that reflect the island's natural abundance.

10. Experiencing the Local Markets:

One of the best ways to immerse yourself in Bora Bora's souvenir and handicraft scene is by exploring the local markets. The main market, Vaitape Market, is a bustling hub where tourists can interact with local vendors and discover an extensive range of products. In addition to the items mentioned earlier, visitors can find traditional Polynesian musical instruments, seashell wind chimes, and handmade baskets, adding to the diverse selection of souvenirs.

Pearl Shops - A Unique Treasure

History of Pearls in Bora Bora:

The love affair between Bora Bora and pearls dates back centuries, with the island's indigenous culture deeply intertwined with pearl harvesting. Natural pearls have been a symbol of wealth, beauty, and luxury throughout history, and Bora Bora's pristine waters are home to the rare and exquisite black pearls, known for their lustrous dark hue.

Bora Bora's pearl industry was given a significant boost in the early 1960s when French Polynesia's government introduced pearl farming techniques from Japan. With the careful cultivation of black-lipped oysters, the lustrous black pearls of Bora Bora have become coveted worldwide. Today, the island's pearl shops showcase an array of exceptional pearls, ranging in size, shape, color, and quality, providing visitors with an opportunity to take home a unique and cherished piece of this paradise.

Types of Pearls Found in Bora Bora:

The prized black pearls of Bora Bora are predominantly cultivated from the Pinctada margaritifera, commonly known as the black-lipped oyster. These remarkable mollusks thrive in the warm, nutrient-rich waters of the South Pacific and produce pearls with a distinctive dark sheen.

Bora Bora's pearl shops offer an array of pearl varieties, including:

Black Pearls: These pearls showcase a spectrum of colors ranging from peacock green to midnight black. They are the most sought-after and are often considered a symbol of elegance and prestige.

White Pearls: While black pearls take center stage, Bora Bora also offers stunning white pearls. White pearls emanate a timeless beauty and are perfect for those seeking a classic look.

Champagne Pearls: Champagne pearls boast a warm, golden hue, exuding a sense of sophistication and charm.

Tahitian Pearls: Tahitian pearls are synonymous with Bora Bora, as they are cultivated in the surrounding waters of French Polynesia. They are highly coveted for their unique colors and large size.

Baroque Pearls: These naturally irregular-shaped pearls embrace an organic and artistic allure.

Popular Pearl Shops in Bora Bora:

Bora Bora is home to a diverse range of pearl shops, each offering its own distinct collection and shopping experience. Some of the most renowned pearl shops that visitors should explore include:

Maison de la Perle: One of the most famous pearl shops on the island, Maison de la Perle, is located in Vaitape, the main village of Bora Bora. The boutique showcases an impressive assortment of pearls, from classic designs to exquisite high-end jewelry.

Robert Wan Pearl Museum: Not just a pearl shop, but an entire museum dedicated to the fascinating world of pearls. Here, visitors can learn about the history of pearl farming and appreciate an extensive collection of pearls.

Black Pearl Bora Bora: Situated in Matira Beach, this pearl shop is renowned for its warm and welcoming ambiance. Visitors can enjoy personalized service while browsing an enticing selection of pearls.

Pearl Romance: Nestled on the water's edge, Pearl Romance offers visitors a picturesque setting to explore stunning pearl jewelry while enjoying breathtaking views of Bora Bora's crystal-clear lagoon.

Motu Pearl Farm: For those seeking a more immersive experience, Motu Pearl Farm provides guided tours that showcase the pearl cultivation process. Visitors can witness the pearl grafting and harvesting techniques, gaining insight into this labor of love.

Selecting the Perfect Pearl:

Choosing the ideal pearl is a thrilling adventure in itself. Here are some essential tips to help visitors find their perfect gem:

Luster: Look for pearls with a brilliant, mirror-like luster. A high-quality pearl will reflect light, adding an alluring glow to the gem.

Shape: Pearls come in various shapes, including round, semi-round, drop, and **baroque.** Round pearls are considered the most valuable, but each shape possesses its own unique charm.

Color: Embrace the opportunity to explore the vast array of pearl colors, from deep black to soft pastels. Choose a hue that resonates with your personal style and preferences.

Surface Quality: Examine the surface of the pearl for any imperfections. While slight blemishes are common, select pearls with minimal flaws for a more exquisite piece.

Size: Consider the size of the pearl and how it complements your style and body proportions. Larger pearls often make a bold statement, while smaller ones can be delicate and elegant.

Pearl Care and Certification:

Once you've found your perfect pearl, it's essential to care for it properly to maintain its beauty for generations. Pearls are organic gems and require delicate handling. Avoid exposing them to harsh chemicals, extreme temperatures, or direct sunlight. Instead, gently clean them with a soft, damp cloth to remove any residue.

When purchasing pearls, inquire about the shop's certification process. Reputable pearl shops provide certificates of authenticity, detailing the pearl's origin, quality, and any treatments it may have undergone.

Local Markets

The Enchanting World of Bora Bora's Local Markets

As you step foot onto this idyllic island, you'll immediately be drawn to the lively atmosphere of its local markets. Located in various neighborhoods, these markets serve as a hub of activity where locals and visitors alike come together to trade, socialize, and celebrate the rich island culture. Exploring these markets is a wonderful way to experience the real essence of Bora Bora beyond the glossy brochures and postcard-perfect views.

Discovering the Flavors of Bora Bora: Food Markets

One of the highlights of visiting local markets in Bora Bora is the opportunity to savor a diverse range of fresh, local produce. Food markets are abundant on the island, offering an array of tropical fruits, vegetables, and aromatic spices that are unique to the region. The main food market in the town of Vaitape is a bustling hub of activity where you can interact with local farmers and sample traditional dishes.

a. Fresh Tropical Fruits: Pineapples, coconuts, papayas, bananas, and passion fruit are just a few of the tropical delights that await you at the markets. Vendors often offer fresh fruit juices and smoothies, providing a refreshing treat in the island's warm climate.

b. Exquisite Seafood: Bora Bora's markets also boast an impressive selection of seafood, caught daily by local fishermen. Fresh fish, such as tuna, mahi-mahi, and parrotfish, are displayed in vibrant arrays, tempting visitors to indulge in the island's culinary treasures.

c. Local Delicacies: Don't miss the chance to try the local specialties, like poisson cru (raw fish marinated in coconut milk and lime) and fafa (cooked taro leaves with coconut milk and meat). These dishes offer a glimpse into the island's unique gastronomy.

Immerse in Culture: Handicraft Markets

For those seeking authentic and unique souvenirs, handicraft markets in Bora Bora are a treasure trove of local artistry and craftsmanship. Local artisans display their creations, reflecting the island's rich cultural heritage and artistic traditions.

a. Traditional Pareos: The colorful and versatile pareo, a traditional Polynesian wrap, is a must-buy souvenir. Hand-painted with vibrant patterns and designs, pareos can be worn as clothing, used as a beach towel, or hung as a decorative piece.

b. Woodcarvings: Intricately carved wooden sculptures and figurines showcase the skill and artistry of Bora Bora's craftsmen. From tiki statues to exquisite masks, these pieces capture the spirit of Polynesian culture.

c. Pearl Jewelry: Bora Bora is renowned for its exquisite pearls, and the markets are the perfect place to find unique jewelry pieces made from these lustrous gems. Whether you seek a classic pearl necklace or a contemporary design, you'll be spoiled for choice.

Exploring Local Traditions: Arts and Crafts Markets

Aside from food and handicraft markets, Bora Bora also hosts arts and crafts markets, which provide an opportunity to witness local artists and performers showcasing their talents.

a. Traditional Dance Performances: These markets often feature lively dance performances, with dancers adorned in colorful costumes, moving to the rhythm of traditional Tahitian drums. Witnessing these performances is an enchanting experience that allows visitors to immerse themselves in the island's cultural heritage.

b. Ukuleles and Instruments: Music is an integral part of Polynesian culture, and you can find beautifully crafted ukuleles and other musical instruments at these markets. Whether you're a musician or simply a lover of music, these instruments make for captivating souvenirs.

Tips for Visiting Local Markets in Bora Bora

a. Timing: Local markets are usually held in the mornings, so arrive early to enjoy the freshest produce and the best selection of handicrafts.

b. Bargaining: Bargaining is a common practice in Bora Bora's markets, especially at the handicraft stalls. Polite and friendly negotiation can often lead to better deals, but remember to be respectful of the local customs.

c. Cash and Currency: While credit cards may be accepted in some markets, it's advisable to carry cash in local currency (CFP Franc) for smoother transactions.

d. Respect Local Customs: Bora Bora's culture is deeply rooted in tradition, so it's essential to respect local customs and show appreciation for the island's heritage during your market visits.

CHAPTER EIGHT:NIGHTLIFE AND ENTERTAINMENT

Bars and Beachfront Hangouts

1. Matira Beach Bar

Nestled along the iconic Matira Beach, the Matira Beach Bar is a must-visit spot for travelers seeking a casual and laid-back atmosphere. With its bamboo décor, palm-thatched roof, and stunning views of the Pacific Ocean, the bar perfectly captures the essence of island life. Visitors can unwind with a refreshing cocktail while sinking their toes into the soft, powdery sand. The Matira Beach Bar is an excellent spot to witness the breathtaking sunsets that Bora Bora is famous for, making it a popular hangout spot for locals and tourists alike.

2. Bloody Mary's

Bloody Mary's is an iconic and legendary bar located in the heart of Bora Bora. Known for its quirky decor and signature cocktails, this beachfront hangout has attracted numerous celebrities over the years. Visitors can indulge in a wide selection of fresh seafood, including their famous "Bora Bora Bloody Mary" cocktail, which is made with local ingredients and is a favorite among patrons. The laid-back atmosphere and friendly staff make Bloody Mary's a top choice for an authentic island experience.

3. La Plantation Restaurant and Bar

Located on the Vaitape Harbor, La Plantation Restaurant and Bar offer a refined setting for visitors looking to experience fine dining with a touch of local charm. The bar features a vast selection of wines and handcrafted cocktails, making it an excellent spot to unwind after a day of exploring the island. The waterfront view and romantic ambiance create an unforgettable setting for couples seeking a memorable evening.

4. Bora Bora Yacht Club

The Bora Bora Yacht Club is a lively beachfront hangout that caters to both yacht enthusiasts and tourists. The bar offers a wide range of tropical cocktails and hosts live music events, transforming the venue into a vibrant and energetic space. Whether visitors arrive by boat or simply stroll in from the nearby beach, the Bora Bora Yacht Club provides a unique and memorable experience.

5. The St. Regis Bar

Situated within the luxurious St. Regis Bora Bora Resort, The St. Regis Bar offers an upscale and sophisticated ambiance for those seeking a more refined setting. With stunning views of Mount Otemanu and the lagoon, visitors can enjoy expertly crafted cocktails while relaxing in plush surroundings. The bar also hosts live entertainment, including traditional Polynesian performances, adding an authentic touch to the experience.

6. Sharky's Bar

Sharky's Bar, located near Matira Beach, is a favorite hangout spot for divers and water sports enthusiasts.

The bar's unique design incorporates a vintage shark cage, creating a quirky and captivating atmosphere. Sharky's offers a selection of tropical drinks and ice-cold beers, making it an ideal spot to unwind and share tales of underwater adventures.

7. Māhāna Beach Bar

Māhāna Beach Bar, situated within the InterContinental Bora Bora Resort & Thalasso Spa, offers a perfect blend of luxury and laid-back vibes. Visitors can enjoy a range of cocktails and snacks while lounging on comfortable beachside seating. The bar's serene and tranquil setting makes it an excellent spot to enjoy the mesmerizing turquoise waters of the lagoon.

Traditional Dance Shows

Historical Background of Traditional Dance in Bora Bora

The traditional dance of Bora Bora, like other Polynesian dances, has a deep-rooted history dating back centuries. Polynesian dance is believed to have evolved from ancient rituals and ceremonies, serving as a form of storytelling, entertainment, and spiritual expression. These dances were an integral part of the community's social and cultural fabric, conveying myths, legends, and daily life events. Over time, the dances in Bora Bora evolved to reflect the island's unique identity, incorporating elements from its natural surroundings and cultural exchanges with other Pacific islands.

Types of Traditional Dances in Bora Bora

Bora Bora's dance repertoire comprises various dance styles, each with its distinct significance and choreographic elements. Here are some of the most prominent traditional dances performed in the island:

1. 'Ote'a: Also known as the 'ote'a drum dance, this high-energy, rhythmic performance is one of the most iconic dances in Bora Bora. Dancers, both male and female, adorned in colorful costumes, sway their hips, stomp their feet, and move in unison to the beat of drums, conch shells, and traditional instruments. 'Ote'a is often performed during celebrations, festivals, and special occasions, evoking a sense of unity, strength, and pride among the performers and the audience.

2. 'Aparima: In contrast to the lively 'ote'a, 'aparima is a slower, more graceful dance that emphasizes hand and arm movements. The dance often depicts stories of love, nature, and everyday life experiences. Dancers use graceful gestures and symbolic movements to portray emotions and narratives, accompanied by melodious songs that further enhance the performance's emotional depth.

3. Hivinau: Hivinau is a dance that showcases the skill and strength of the male performers. It involves feats of strength and athleticism, as men execute complex movements and lift heavy objects during the dance. This dance embodies the spirit of masculinity, with participants displaying their physical prowess and agility.

4. Hura: Hura is a traditional dance form performed during Tahitian weddings. This joyous dance celebrates love and union, with couples or groups of dancers swaying and moving in harmony, expressing their happiness and excitement for the newlyweds.

Importance of Dance in Bora Bora's Culture

Dance is an integral part of Bora Bora's culture, reflecting the islanders' strong connection with their past, ancestors, and environment. Traditional dance holds deep cultural significance and serves multiple purposes within the community:

1. Cultural Preservation: Traditional dance acts as a vessel for preserving and passing on Bora Bora's rich cultural heritage to future generations. By practicing and performing these dances, the islanders ensure that their customs, stories, and values remain alive and relevant.

2. Celebration of Identity: Through dance, the people of Bora Bora express their unique identity and pride in their heritage. Each dance embodies specific elements of the island's history and showcases the distinct characteristics that set Bora Bora apart from other Pacific islands.

3. Spiritual Expression: Dance in Bora Bora has deep spiritual roots, and it is often linked to religious or spiritual rituals. These dances were once performed as offerings to gods, ancestors, or natural elements, seeking protection, blessings, or guidance from higher powers.

4. Entertainment and Social Bonding: Dance serves as a form of entertainment and social bonding in the community. Festivals, gatherings, and special occasions provide opportunities for people to come together, enjoy performances, and strengthen their social ties.

Traditional Dance Shows for Visitors

Visitors to Bora Bora have the unique privilege of witnessing these mesmerizing traditional dance shows, which are typically organized by resorts, cultural centers, and local communities. These shows provide tourists with an authentic glimpse into the island's heritage and offer an immersive cultural experience. Here's what visitors can expect from traditional dance shows in Bora Bora:

1. Enchanting Performances: Traditional dance shows feature skilled and passionate dancers adorned in vibrant costumes. The captivating movements, rhythmic beats, and soulful melodies transport the audience to a different world, evoking a sense of wonder and appreciation for Polynesian culture.

2. Cultural Education: These dance shows often include informative narration, where performers explain the significance of each dance and its connection to Bora Bora's history and culture. Visitors gain valuable insights into the island's traditions and the stories behind the dances they are witnessing.

3. Audience Participation: Many traditional dance shows encourage audience participation, allowing visitors to learn basic dance steps and join in the festivities. This interactive element enhances the overall experience, fostering a sense of camaraderie between locals and tourists.

4. Craft and Art Displays: In addition to the dance performances, visitors may also have the opportunity to explore craft and art displays showcasing traditional Polynesian arts, handicrafts, and souvenirs. These displays further enrich the cultural experience and provide opportunities to support local artisans.

Stargazing and Nighttime Activities

. The Celestial Splendor of Bora Bora's Night Sky

Bora Bora is situated far away from major urban centers, resulting in minimal light pollution. As a result, the island offers visitors a clear and uninterrupted view of the celestial wonders above. On a clear night, stargazers can witness the Milky Way stretching across the sky, constellations glittering in their full glory, and shooting stars dashing across the horizon. The island's geographic location near the equator grants visibility to both the northern and southern hemispheres, providing a unique opportunity to see stars from different constellations.

A. Optimal Stargazing Spots

Matira Beach: Matira Beach is one of the most popular stargazing spots on the island. Visitors can lay down on the soft, sandy shore, relax, and look up to witness the breathtaking night sky unfold above them. The absence of city lights in the area makes Matira Beach an ideal location to appreciate the stars.

Mount Otemanu: For the more adventurous stargazers, hiking up Mount Otemanu is a rewarding experience. As the highest point on the island, it offers an unparalleled panoramic view of the night sky. It is recommended to undertake this activity with a guide for safety and to fully enjoy the journey.

Overwater Bungalows: Many of Bora Bora's luxurious resorts offer overwater bungalows with direct access to the lagoon. These accommodations provide a private and intimate setting for stargazing right from the comfort of your own deck.

II. Stargazing Tours and Astronomy Excursions

To enhance the stargazing experience, several local tour operators offer astronomy excursions and stargazing tours that are tailored to both amateur and experienced stargazers. These guided tours provide insights into the celestial world while allowing visitors to use state-of-the-art telescopes and astronomical equipment.

A. Bora Bora Astronomy Tours: Bora Bora Astronomy Tours is a reputable company that organizes stargazing excursions for small groups. Led by experienced astronomers, these tours offer engaging discussions about celestial bodies, mythology, and Polynesian navigation techniques.

B. Stargazing Catamaran Cruises: For a romantic and memorable experience, couples can embark on a stargazing catamaran cruise. As the catamaran glides smoothly across the lagoon, passengers can enjoy the night sky while savoring a sumptuous dinner and tropical drinks.

C. Nighttime Helicopter Tours: For a more unique perspective, visitors can take a nighttime helicopter tour that soars above the island and provides an awe-inspiring view of the stars from a higher altitude. These tours are particularly popular during meteor showers and other astronomical events.

III. Bora Bora's Cultural Night Activities

Apart from stargazing, Bora Bora offers a variety of cultural nighttime activities that allow visitors to immerse themselves in the local Polynesian traditions and entertainment.

A. Traditional Polynesian Dance Shows: Many resorts and restaurants on the island host traditional

Polynesian dance shows in the evening. These performances showcase the vibrant culture of French Polynesia through dance, music, and colorful costumes. Visitors can enjoy the rhythmic beats and graceful movements of dancers under the starlit sky.

B. Beach Bonfires and Tahitian Drumming: Some resorts organize beach bonfires accompanied by Tahitian drumming sessions. This laid-back and interactive experience provides a perfect setting to relax, socialize, and embrace the tranquil atmosphere of the island at night.

C. Nighttime Lagoon Tours: Guided lagoon tours during the night offer a magical opportunity to witness bioluminescent plankton glowing underwater. As visitors paddle through the illuminated lagoon, they are enchanted by the natural spectacle surrounding them.

IV. Astro-Photography in Bora Bora

For photography enthusiasts, Bora Bora provides a fantastic canvas to capture the night sky in all its glory. The combination of the dark skies and the stunning landscape creates the perfect setting for astrophotography.

A. Essential Tips for Astro-Photography:

Use a Tripod: To capture clear and sharp images of the night sky, it is crucial to stabilize the camera on a tripod.

Longer Exposure Times: Long exposure times allow the camera to capture more light from the stars, revealing their intricate details.

Avoid Light Pollution: To ensure high-quality astrophotography, find locations away from artificial lights to avoid any unwanted light pollution.

Bring Wide-Angle Lenses: Wide-angle lenses are ideal for capturing expansive shots of the night sky and its surroundings.

V. Meteorological Considerations and Best Time to Visit

Before planning a stargazing trip to Bora Bora, visitors should be mindful of the weather conditions and astronomical events that might enhance the experience.

A. Dry Season: The dry season, typically lasting from May to October, offers the most stable weather conditions with clear skies, making it the ideal time for stargazing.

B. Meteor Showers: To witness meteor showers, such as the famous Perseids or Geminids, visitors should research the dates of these events and plan their trips accordingly.

C. Moon Phase: The phase of the moon can affect stargazing visibility. A new moon or crescent moon provides darker skies and better stargazing opportunities compared to a full moon, which can be quite bright and obstruct the view of fainter celestial objects.

VI. Respect for Local Environment and Culture

While enjoying stargazing and nighttime activities in Bora Bora, it is essential for visitors to respect the local environment and culture.

A. Light Pollution: To preserve the natural beauty of the night sky, visitors are encouraged to minimize the use of artificial lights during their stay.

B. Local Customs: Embrace and respect the local Polynesian culture, which holds the night sky and celestial objects with deep spiritual significance.

CHAPTER   NINE:PRACTICAL TIPS AND SAFETY

Currency and Payment Methods

Currency in Bora Bora:

The official currency of Bora Bora is the French Pacific Franc (XPF), also known as the CFP Franc. The CFP Franc is the legal tender in several French Overseas Territories, including French Polynesia, New Caledonia, Wallis, and Futuna. The ISO code for the CFP Franc is XPF, and its symbol is "₣" or "F".

The CFP Franc is a fixed currency pegged to the Euro (EUR), with a fixed exchange rate of 1 EUR = 119.33 XPF. This exchange rate has remained stable for years, ensuring a consistent value for the CFP Franc relative to the Euro.

Exchange Rate Considerations:

Before traveling to Bora Bora, it is advisable to check the current exchange rates for the CFP Franc in comparison to your home currency. While the exchange rate with the Euro remains stable, it might fluctuate against other major currencies like the US Dollar or the Japanese Yen. To get the most favorable rate, consider exchanging your money at reputable banks or exchange offices, both at home and in Bora Bora.

Payment Methods Accepted:

Cash: In Bora Bora, cash is widely accepted and often preferred, especially for small transactions, local shops, and markets. It is advisable to carry some cash with you for small expenses and situations where credit cards might not be accepted.

Credit and Debit Cards: Credit and debit cards are commonly accepted at hotels, resorts, high-end restaurants, and major tourist attractions in Bora Bora. Visa and Mastercard are the most widely accepted cards, followed by American Express and Diners Club to a lesser extent. However, it is essential to have some cash on hand, as not all establishments may accept cards, especially in more remote areas.

Traveler's Checks: While traveler's checks used to be a popular option for international travel, their acceptance has significantly declined in recent years. Many establishments no longer accept traveler's checks due to their inconvenience and the prevalence of other payment methods.

Mobile Payment Apps: Depending on the time period, some mobile payment apps might have been introduced in Bora Bora. These apps enable tourists to make payments using their smartphones, but their availability might be limited, and not all merchants may accept them.

Banking Facilities:

Bora Bora offers adequate banking facilities to cater to the needs of tourists. The major towns on the island, such as Vaitape, have banks and ATMs where visitors can withdraw cash and perform essential banking transactions. It is essential to be aware of any potential transaction fees that your home bank may charge for international withdrawals.

In addition to the local banks, some hotels and resorts may also provide currency exchange services for their guests. However, these services might have less favorable exchange rates and higher fees, so it's wise to inquire about the rates and fees before using them.

Practical Tips for Managing Money:

Notify Your Bank: Before traveling to Bora Bora or any international destination, notify your bank of your travel plans. This helps avoid potential issues with your cards being blocked for suspected fraudulent activity when used abroad.

Carry Multiple Payment Methods: To ensure financial flexibility, bring a combination of cash, credit cards, and debit cards. While credit cards offer convenience and security, having some cash on hand can be helpful for smaller transactions and situations where cards are not accepted.

Beware of Dynamic Currency Conversion (DCC): When paying with a credit card, you may encounter the option for Dynamic Currency Conversion, where the merchant offers to convert the transaction amount into your home currency. While this may seem convenient, it often comes with unfavorable exchange rates and additional fees. Opt to pay in the local currency (XPF) to avoid unnecessary charges.

Budget Wisely: Bora Bora is renowned for its luxury and can be an expensive destination.

Plan your budget accordingly, and be mindful of your spending to ensure a memorable and stress-free vacation.

Keep Emergency Cash: While Bora Bora is generally safe for tourists, unexpected situations can occur. It's a good idea to keep some emergency cash securely tucked away in case of any unforeseen circumstances.

Language and Communication

1. The Languages of Bora Bora

Bora Bora is a multilingual society where several languages are spoken, but two primary languages dominate: Tahitian and French. Tahitian, an Austronesian language, is the most widely spoken native language on the island. It is rich in cultural significance and remains a cherished part of the local identity. French, as the official language of French Polynesia, is used in formal settings, government institutions, and schools. While English is not as prevalent, it is often spoken in tourist-centric areas, especially by those involved in the hospitality industry.

2. The Importance of Learning Basic Tahitian Phrases

As a visitor to Bora Bora, making an effort to learn some basic Tahitian phrases can greatly enhance your experience and leave a positive impression on the locals. The Tahitian language is integral to the island's cultural heritage, and using a few key expressions will show respect and appreciation for their traditions. Some essential phrases to learn include greetings like "Ia ora na" (Hello) and "Nana" (Goodbye), as well as polite expressions such as "Mauruuru" (Thank you) and "Māuruuru roa" (Thank you very much).

3. Cultural Communication Norms

In Bora Bora, communication extends beyond mere words; it encompasses gestures, facial expressions, and body language. The locals are known for their warmth and hospitality, so expect to engage in friendly small talk and smiles throughout your interactions. Politeness is highly valued, and maintaining a respectful tone and demeanor is essential, especially when addressing elders or those in positions of authority.

Furthermore, it is customary to maintain eye contact during conversations, as it is seen as a sign of respect and attentiveness. Physical contact, such as handshakes or gentle hugs, may also be used to greet friends and acquaintances. It is important to be mindful of personal space and follow the lead of locals to ensure comfortable interactions.

4. Communicating in Tourism-Centric Areas

In Bora Bora's tourist areas, you can expect a higher level of English proficiency among the locals working in the hospitality industry. Resort staff, tour guides, and vendors often speak English, making it easier for visitors to communicate their needs and preferences.

However, even with English-speaking locals, attempting to use basic Tahitian phrases will be greatly appreciated and may lead to more enriching interactions. Demonstrating an interest in the local language and culture will often result in the locals being more open and eager to share insights and stories with you.

5. Learning from the Local Traditions

Traditional storytelling, dance, and songs are important aspects of Bora Bora's culture. The locals often use these mediums to pass down historical knowledge, teach life lessons, and celebrate their heritage. Engaging in these activities and attending cultural performances not only offers a glimpse into their history but also strengthens the connection between visitors and the local community.

When attending events or ceremonies, it is advisable to observe and follow the lead of others to show respect for the customs and traditions. Keep in mind that some ceremonies may be sacred or reserved for specific occasions, so it's essential to inquire about appropriate behavior beforehand.

6. Overcoming Language Barriers

In certain situations, you may encounter language barriers, especially when interacting with those who do not speak English fluently. In such cases, patience and a friendly attitude are key. Utilize simple gestures, visual aids, or translation apps on your smartphone to bridge the communication gap.

The locals are generally understanding and accommodating, appreciating visitors who make an effort to adapt to their language and communication styles. Don't hesitate to ask for help or clarification; chances are, someone nearby will be more than happy to assist.

Safety Precautions

Water Activities and Marine Safety: Bora Bora is renowned for its stunning lagoon and pristine waters, making water activities a must-do for most visitors. However, it's essential to be aware of potential risks and take appropriate precautions:

- **Snorkeling and Diving:** Before engaging in these activities, ensure that you are familiar with the gear and equipment. Only swim and snorkel in designated safe zones. Pay attention to currents and always follow the instructions of your guide.
- **Shark and Stingray Feeding:** While it's a thrilling experience to encounter sharks and stingrays, this activity should only

be done with reputable tour operators who follow strict safety protocols. Respect the animals' space and never touch or provoke them.

- **Jet Skiing and Water Sports:** Always wear a life jacket while participating in water sports. Pay attention to your surroundings, especially other watercraft, to avoid collisions.
- **Boating and Sailing:** If you rent a boat, ensure you have proper boating experience or hire a licensed captain. Follow navigational rules and regulations, and check the weather conditions before setting sail.

Sun Protection: The tropical climate of Bora Bora means the sun can be intense. Sun protection is essential to prevent sunburn and long-term skin damage:

- **Sunscreen:** Apply a high SPF sunscreen regularly, especially during water activities. Consider using reef-safe sunscreen to protect the delicate marine ecosystem.
- **Sun Hats and Sunglasses:** Wear a wide-brimmed hat and sunglasses to

protect your face and eyes from direct sunlight.

Accommodation Safety: When choosing accommodation in Bora Bora, consider the following safety aspects:

- **Fire Safety:** Ensure that the hotel or resort you select has proper fire safety measures and emergency evacuation plans in place.
- **Security:** Choose reputable accommodations with good security measures to safeguard your belongings.

Local Customs and Culture: Respecting local customs and culture is essential to have a harmonious and enjoyable experience:

- **Dress Code:** While the island is known for its relaxed atmosphere, it's important to dress modestly when visiting local villages or religious sites.
- **Language:** Learn a few basic French or Tahitian phrases to communicate with the locals and show respect for their culture.
- **Gifts and Tipping:** It's customary to offer a small gift as a token of appreciation when invited into a local's

home. Tipping is not mandatory, but it's appreciated for exceptional service.

Health and Medical Considerations: Ensuring good health during your trip to Bora Bora involves a few precautionary measures:

- **Vaccinations:** Check with your healthcare provider for any recommended vaccinations before traveling.
- **Drinking Water:** Stick to bottled water and avoid drinking tap water to prevent waterborne illnesses.
- **Medical Facilities:** Familiarize yourself with the location of medical facilities on the island in case of emergencies.
- **Insect Protection:** Bring insect repellent and wear appropriate clothing to protect yourself from mosquito bites, which could transmit diseases like dengue fever.

Transportation Safety: Whether you're exploring the island by land or water, transportation safety should be a priority:

- **Driving:** If you plan to rent a car or scooter, ensure you have the necessary licenses and insurance coverage. Drive cautiously, as roads can be narrow and winding.

- **Taxi Safety:** Use licensed and reputable taxi services to ensure your safety during travel.
- **Public Transportation:** If you use public transportation, keep an eye on your belongings to prevent theft.

Emergency Contacts: Before you begin your journey to Bora Bora, make sure you have important emergency contact numbers, including local authorities, medical facilities, and your country's embassy or consulate.

Weather Awareness: Stay updated on the weather forecast and be prepared for sudden changes, especially during hurricane season (November to April).

Travel Insurance: Consider purchasing travel insurance that covers medical emergencies, trip cancellations, and other unforeseen incidents.

Respecting Wildlife: Bora Bora is home to unique and diverse wildlife, including marine animals and bird species. Always observe animals from a safe distance, and avoid disturbing their natural habitat.

CHAPTER TEN:DAY TRIPS TO SURROUNDING ISLANDS

Tahiti - The Heart of French Polynesia

French Polynesia: A Quick Overview

French Polynesia is an overseas collectivity of France located in the South Pacific Ocean. It consists of 118 islands, each unique in its beauty and charm. Among the most famous and beloved of these is Bora Bora, known for its luxurious overwater bungalows and stunning coral reefs, and Tahiti, the largest and most populous island in the archipelago, where the vibrant capital city of Papeete is situated.

Preparation for the Day Trip

Before embarking on your day trip from Bora Bora to Tahiti, there are a few essential preparations to make. Ensure you have your passport, identification, and any necessary travel documents, as French Polynesia is an overseas territory of France. Additionally, pack light, bringing essentials such as sunscreen, a hat, comfortable footwear for walking, a camera, and a water bottle.

Morning: Departure from Bora Bora

The day begins with an early morning departure from Bora Bora. Head to the Vaitape Harbor, where you'll find boats and ferries that offer regular trips to Tahiti. Choose between various transportation options, including high-speed catamarans and traditional Polynesian outrigger canoes. The journey between Bora Bora and Tahiti takes approximately 4 to 5 hours, depending on your chosen mode of transportation.

En Route: Embrace the Scenic Beauty

As your boat glides across the azure waters, take a moment to soak in the awe-inspiring scenery surrounding you. The view of Bora Bora's iconic Mount Otemanu slowly fading into the horizon is an unforgettable sight. Keep your eyes peeled for dolphins and flying fish dancing alongside the boat, creating a delightful spectacle.

Arrival in Tahiti: Exploring Papeete

Upon reaching the capital city of Papeete, you'll be welcomed by the lively sounds of Tahitian music and the vibrant atmosphere of the bustling marketplace. Spend some time exploring the vibrant city, starting with a visit to the famous Papeete Market. Here, you'll find an array of local produce, tropical fruits, artisanal crafts, and intricate black pearls—Tahiti's precious gems.

Discovering the Black Pearl

Tahiti is renowned for its exquisite black pearls, often referred to as "Tahitian pearls." These pearls are a symbol of the island's cultural heritage and are highly coveted worldwide. Consider taking a guided tour of a pearl farm to learn about the cultivation process and the fascinating history of these jewels. You may even have the opportunity to purchase a unique black pearl souvenir to remember your journey forever.

Cultural Experience: Le Musée de Tahiti et des Îles

To delve deeper into the rich culture and history of French Polynesia, head to Le Musée de Tahiti et des Îles (The Museum of Tahiti and the Islands). This museum houses an extensive collection of artifacts, art, and historical exhibits that shed light on the region's past, including the migration patterns of Polynesians, the arrival of Europeans, and the significance of the islands' flora and fauna.

Lunch: Savoring Tahitian Cuisine

No visit to Tahiti is complete without indulging in the island's delectable cuisine. For lunch, head to one of Papeete's charming waterfront restaurants, where you can enjoy a variety of dishes inspired by the fusion of French and Polynesian culinary traditions. Savor the delicate flavors of Poisson Cru, a traditional raw fish dish marinated in lime juice and coconut milk, or relish a hearty meal of Poulet Fafa, a succulent chicken dish cooked with taro leaves.

Afternoon: Island Excursion

As the day progresses, venture outside of Papeete to explore some of Tahiti's natural wonders. A popular destination is the Fautaua Valley, home to the impressive Fautaua Waterfall. Hike through lush vegetation to reach the waterfall's base, where you can enjoy the refreshing mist and marvel at the lush surroundings. Alternatively, opt for a guided tour to the Papenoo Valley, where rugged landscapes, roaring rivers, and ancient archaeological sites await.

Beach Bliss: La Plage de Maui

For those seeking a more relaxed afternoon, make your way to the serene La Plage de Maui. This beautiful beach, located on Tahiti's southern coast, offers soft, white sands and clear waters—a perfect spot to unwind and take in the breathtaking views of the Pacific Ocean. Whether you choose to swim, sunbathe, or simply read a book under the swaying palm trees, La Plage de Maui promises a tranquil and rejuvenating experience.

Evening: Sunset Farewell

As the sun begins to set over Tahiti's horizon, take a moment to reflect on the memorable day you've had. With the golden hues of the sky reflecting upon the lagoon, you'll understand why the magic of French Polynesia has captivated travelers for generations. Bid farewell to Tahiti and board your boat back to

Bora Bora with a heart full of cherished memories and a desire to return someday.

Moorea - A Gem of the Society Islands

I. Getting Ready for the Journey:

Transportation Options: To embark on the day trip from Bora Bora to Moorea, visitors have two primary transportation options: air and sea. Air travel, while faster, may be limited in availability and might not offer the same scenic experience as a boat journey. On the other hand, a boat ride, such as a ferry or private boat charter, allows travelers to savor the magnificent landscapes of the archipelago along the way.

Preparations and Essentials: Before starting the day trip, visitors are advised to pack essential items such as sunscreen, hats, sunglasses, swimwear, towels, and a camera to capture the mesmerizing moments. It is crucial to check the weather forecast and sea conditions to ensure a safe and enjoyable journey.

II. Setting Sail: Departing Bora Bora:

Early Morning Departure: The day trip commences with an early morning departure from Bora Bora. As the sun rises, casting a golden hue over the island's lush greenery and iconic overwater bungalows, visitors bid farewell to the paradise they have come to adore.

Cruising the Turquoise Waters: The boat glides through the turquoise waters of the Pacific Ocean, offering stunning vistas of Bora Bora's iconic Mount Otemanu and the surrounding atolls. The sea breeze caresses the skin, and the scent of the ocean fills the air, setting the tone for an unforgettable day ahead.

III. Arriving in Moorea: Unveiling the Hidden Paradise:

Moorea's Panoramic Beauty: After a picturesque journey, the boat docks at Moorea's pier, where travelers are greeted by the awe-inspiring sight of the island's verdant mountains and jagged peaks. Often referred to as "The Magical Island," Moorea's beauty surpasses even the wildest imaginations.

Exploring Belvedere Lookout: The first stop in Moorea is the Belvedere Lookout, located high in the volcanic hills. This vantage point offers panoramic views of Cook's Bay and Opunohu Bay, providing an excellent opportunity for visitors to capture breathtaking photographs. The lush vegetation and vibrant flora only enhance the allure of the landscape.

Admiring Pineapple Plantations: Next, the day trip ventures to Moorea's pineapple plantations, where visitors can witness the island's agricultural side. Here, tourists can savor the sweet and juicy tropical fruit, fresh from the fields, while learning about the local farming techniques that sustain the island's economy.

IV. Immersing in Marine Wonders:

Lagoon and Coral Garden Exploration: No trip to Moorea would be complete without diving into its mesmerizing lagoon and exploring the vibrant coral gardens beneath the surface.

Snorkeling and swimming in the clear waters reveal a kaleidoscope of colorful marine life, including tropical fish, rays, and maybe even a glimpse of a friendly reef shark. Under the guidance of experienced guides, visitors can safely interact with the marine wonders, leaving them in awe of the untouched beauty. **Dolphin and Whale Watching:** Moorea is also renowned for its opportunities to observe marine mammals. Depending on the time of year, lucky visitors might spot playful dolphins or majestic humpback whales migrating through these waters. Guided tours ensure that these experiences are respectful and non-intrusive, promoting responsible tourism practices.

V. Embracing the Culture:

Tahitian Dance Performances: As part of the day trip, visitors can immerse themselves in the vibrant Tahitian culture by witnessing traditional dance performances. These captivating displays often feature rhythmic drumming and gracefully choreographed movements, giving travelers an insight into the island's rich heritage.

Experiencing Local Cuisine: The day trip also provides ample opportunities to savor the unique flavors of Moorea. Local restaurants and food stalls offer a range of tantalizing dishes, from fresh seafood to tropical fruits, allowing visitors to indulge in the authentic tastes of Polynesian cuisine.

VI. The Return to Bora Bora:

As the sun begins to set over Moorea's horizon, the day trip draws to a close. The return journey to Bora Bora allows visitors to reflect on the unforgettable experiences they have had in this hidden paradise. The tranquility of the sea voyage offers a chance to soak in the magic of both islands, leaving travelers with lasting memories that will stay with them forever.

Raiatea and Taha'a - Cultural Encounters

Departure from Bora Bora to Raiatea

The journey begins at the Vaitape Harbor on Bora Bora, where travelers embark on a scenic boat ride to Raiatea. As the boat glides across the crystalline waters, guests are treated to awe-inspiring views of Bora Bora's iconic Mount Otemanu and the surrounding coral reefs, teeming with vibrant marine life. The azure skies overhead and the gentle ocean breeze create a sense of tranquility, setting the stage for a day filled with exploration and adventure.

Raiatea - The Sacred Island

After a leisurely boat ride, visitors arrive at Raiatea, the second-largest island in French Polynesia and often referred to as "The Sacred Island." Raiatea's rich cultural significance is deeply rooted in Polynesian mythology and is considered the ancestral homeland of the Polynesians. Here, travelers have the opportunity to immerse themselves in the island's history and natural beauty.

Taputapuatea Marae: A Journey into Ancient History

The first stop is the Taputapuatea Marae, an ancient religious site and a UNESCO World Heritage site. This sacred complex is an essential pilgrimage site for

Polynesians, reflecting the cultural and spiritual importance of Raiatea in the region. Visitors can explore the intricately carved stone platforms and towering tikis while learning about the ancient rituals and customs that took place here.

Faaroa River: A Serene Canoe Expedition

Next, travelers venture to the Faaroa River, the only navigable river in French Polynesia. Surrounded by lush vegetation and vibrant flora, the river offers a serene canoeing experience. Guests paddle along the winding waterways, enjoying the verdant landscape and perhaps catching glimpses of exotic birds and aquatic life that call this area home.

Uturoa Market: A Gastronomic Delight

For those seeking an authentic taste of Raiatean culture, a visit to the bustling Uturoa Market is a must. Local vendors display an array of fresh fruits, fragrant vanilla beans, and handcrafted souvenirs. Travelers can indulge in freshly prepared tropical delicacies while mingling with friendly locals, creating an immersive cultural experience.

Taha'a - The Vanilla Island

Leaving Raiatea behind, the day trip continues to Taha'a, a small but captivating island often referred to as "The Vanilla Island." Taha'a is renowned for its vanilla plantations, fragrant flower-scented air, and mesmerizing coral gardens.

Vanilla Plantations: A Whiff of Perfumed Delight

Upon arrival in Taha'a, visitors are greeted by the delightful aroma of vanilla, which is grown in abundance on the island. Travelers can take guided tours of the vanilla plantations, learning about the intricate process of pollination and cultivation that goes into producing the world's most sought-after vanilla beans. Sampling freshly made vanilla-infused products is a memorable treat for the senses.

Coral Garden Snorkeling: An Underwater Wonderland

No visit to Taha'a would be complete without exploring its enchanting coral gardens. With crystal-clear waters and diverse marine life, Taha'a offers excellent snorkeling opportunities. Travelers are awestruck by the kaleidoscope of colors presented by the vibrant coral reefs and the dazzling array of tropical fish that inhabit these underwater wonderlands.

Private Motu Picnic: A Secluded Paradise

To enhance the day's adventure, guests can opt for a private motu picnic. Motus are small islets scattered around the main islands, and Taha'a has some particularly picturesque ones. A picnic on a secluded motu provides a glimpse of paradise, with soft, powdery sand, swaying palm trees, and a sumptuous spread of local cuisine.

Made in the USA
Columbia, SC
30 October 2024